SANDBOXING IN PRACTICE

Creative Research Methods in Practice

Series Editor: **Helen Kara**, We Research It Ltd.

This dynamic series presents short practical books by and for researchers around the world on how to use creative and innovative research methods from apps to zines. Edited by the leading independent researcher Helen Kara, it is the first series to provide guidance on using creative research methods across all disciplines.

Also available in the series:

- *Encountering the World with I-Docs* by Ella Harris
- *Doing Phenomenography* by Amanda Taylor-Beswick and Eva Hornung
- *Fiction and Research* by Becky Tipper and Leah Gilman
- *Photovoice Reimagined* by Nicole Brown

Find out more at:
policy.bristoluniversitypress.co.uk/
creative-research-methods-in-practice

SANDBOXING IN PRACTICE

Qualitative Interviewing with
Sand, Objects, and Figures

Dawn Mannay and Victoria Timperley

With a foreword by
Debbie Watson

First published in Great Britain in 2025 by

Policy Press, an imprint of
Bristol University Press
University of Bristol
1–9 Old Park Hill
Bristol
BS2 8BB
UK
t: +44 (0)117 374 6645
e: bup-info@bristol.ac.uk

Details of international sales and distribution partners are available at
policy.bristoluniversitypress.co.uk

© Bristol University Press 2025

British Library Cataloguing in Publication Data
A catalogue record for this book is available from the British Library

ISBN 978-1-4473-7290-5 hardcover
ISBN 978-1-4473-7291-2 paperback
ISBN 978-1-4473-7292-9 ePub
ISBN 978-1-4473-7293-6 ePdf

The right of Dawn Mannay and Victoria Timperley to be identified as authors of this work has been asserted by them in accordance with the Copyright, Designs and Patents Act 1988.

All rights reserved: no part of this publication may be reproduced, stored in a retrieval system, or transmitted in any form or by any means, electronic, mechanical, photocopying, recording, or otherwise without the prior permission of Bristol University Press.

Every reasonable effort has been made to obtain permission to reproduce copyrighted material. If, however, anyone knows of an oversight, please contact the publisher.

The statements and opinions contained within this publication are solely those of the authors and not of the University of Bristol or Bristol University Press. The University of Bristol and Bristol University Press disclaim responsibility for any injury to persons or property resulting from any material published in this publication.

Bristol University Press and Policy Press work to counter discrimination on grounds of gender, race, disability, age and sexuality.

Cover design: Qube Design
Front cover image: iStock/Veronika Oliinyk

We dedicate this book in memory of Dr Catherine Thomas, whose work could well have contributed to a book in the Creative Research Methods in Practice series had she not been unexpectedly taken by illness.

We hope a little bit of Catherine's creative spirit is communicated in this book.

Contents

List of figures and tables viii
Acknowledgements ix
Foreword by Debbie Watson xi

1	Introduction	1
2	Sandboxing: from therapeutic practice to qualitative data generation	9
3	Sandboxing in practice	33
4	Sandboxing: adaptions and developments	57
5	Conclusion	77

Notes 87
References 89
Index 103

List of figures and tables

Figures

1.1	Sandboxing this book	4
3.1	Confronting barriers	36
3.2	'Slay the class dragon'	37
3.3	Positive aspects	38
3.4	'Swamped' by work	38
3.5	Comparing visiting provision	45
4.1	'No man's land'	60
4.2	'It springs from your box'	64
4.3	Figure with cutlass sword	65
4.4	Tinkerbell	66
4.5	Size differences in sets of figures	68
4.6	'I want to help them'	73
5.1	Reflecting on sandboxing this book	78

Tables

2.1	Inventory of sand box objects – Vicky	22
2.2	Inventory of sand box objects – Dawn	23

Acknowledgements

There are many people who should be thanked and acknowledged for the role they played in the development of *Sandboxing in Practice: Qualitative Interviewing with Sand, Objects, and Figures*.

We are thankful for the invitation from Dr Helen Kara to contribute to the Creative Research Methods in Practice Policy Press series. As series editor, Helen felt that a book showcasing sandboxing would be a welcome addition to this series and it is her interest in the method and her belief in, and support of, us as authors that has enabled us to write this book – thank you, Helen.

We are grateful to the commissioning, editorial, production, and marketing team at Policy Press for their guidance throughout the process of bringing the book to completion. We could not have produced this book without the support of our editor at Policy Press, Paul Stevens, Assistant Editor, Isobel Green, and their colleagues, and Polly Chester, Desk Editor at Bourchier, whose input has been essential in preparing the manuscript for publication. We are also appreciative of the recommendations from the anonymous reviewers who have helped us to refine our content, communication, and coherence.

It is also important to thank all the researchers, participants, practitioners, and students that we have worked with, who have inspired us in different ways, offered ideas, and engaged with us in informal discussions that have been central in bringing this book to completion. We are particularly appreciative of all the colleagues we have worked with in projects featuring sandboxing and the doctoral students and researchers who have not only taken sandboxing on board but also taken it in new and exciting directions.

Additionally, we are grateful to those who have provided permission for us to include photographs of sand scenes from their studies in this book, namely Professor Alyson Rees, Professor Debbie Watson, Dr Catt Turney, and Rhiannon Maniatt.

Lastly, we would like to thank all our great colleagues, friends, and family and in particular those that are most involved in our everyday lives for their loving presence and enduring support. On this basis, Dawn would like to thank David, Jamie, Jordon, Osian, Sherelle, Tahlia, Taya, Tilleah, Tim, Toyah, Travis, and Travis Jay. Vicky would like to thank Tirion, Rhin, Dai, Dawn, Alex, Pika, and Tank.

Foreword

Debbie Watson, Professor of Child and Family Welfare, University of Bristol

In this engaging and accessible book Dawn Mannay and Vicky Timperley take the reader on a journey of how they have explored and developed what is known as the 'sandboxing method'. It is a book designed to demystify the 'how to' of this approach and to encourage readers to experiment and adapt. I particularly appreciated the generosity of the writing in respect of sharing their uncertainties and concerns as well as recognising that there is no one 'correct' way of sandboxing. I can see this book being valued by researchers from many different disciplines and at different stages of their research careers.

As someone who has used sandboxing, I valued the focus on rooting methodological uses of sand and objects in Indigenous practices and therapy and the authors' thoughtful critique of the crossovers and tensions between therapy and research. Many arts-based research methods utilised in qualitative research have been used in therapeutic contexts with inevitable concern expressed by some people about their use in 'untrained hands'. These are issues well explored in the book and the authors provide future researchers with some useful distinctions and defence to critics.

There are of course deep ethical considerations involved in any research and I believe that utilising objects, metaphors, and the material affordances of sand can give rise to strong emotions and experiences being shared. The authors are sensitive to these ethical challenges, and I particularly welcomed the focus on the protection of researcher wellbeing. In my use of sandboxing, there were difficult times when people reflected on the depths of what they had been able to share through the method and how this would not have been possible in a standard interview. My study involved stories of child abuse which, as researchers, we had to find ways of processing, supporting each other and retaining perspective on our researcher role. For me, this is about being human in research encounters, but such experiences can take an emotional toll, and we need to be prepared for how to support research teams.

Linked to this reflexive positioning of the researcher, the authors describe times when they as researchers have engaged with participants in communal sandboxing; for example, researchers creating sand scenes and being happy to answer questions on these with children. Some great examples are provided and excellent advice for researchers to be participants in their methods and this is certainly something I will carry forward into any further studies with sandboxing.

The focus in the book on the materiality of the method is refreshing. Provision of lists of objects used in studies and consideration of how these have been adapted enable readers to see the flexibility and possibilities of the method. Challenging gender stereotypes through the inclusion of art materials so that participants can augment their characters seems particularly exciting. Similarly, when I used sandboxing, it seemed natural to offer water as a possibility to mould and shape the sand, but I understand the challenges of this despite the remembering of malleable sand on beaches, in nurseries, sandpits, and times playing in and with it.

I highly recommend this book whether you have used sandboxing before or are curious to find out more. It has provoked me to think about my uses of the method and made me appreciate how much I could extend the approach in future studies. The authors write with openness that encourages all of us to continue to reflect, learn, and be generous with our ideas.

1

Introduction

Chapter summary

This short introductory chapter serves as an outline to the book. We begin by sharing our personal sandboxing journeys, before explaining the aims of the book and its intended audiences. The chapter then offers the reader a succinct overview of the following chapters as an orientation to what is to come and what this book has to offer for readers interested in *Qualitative Interviewing with Sand, Objects, and Figures*.

Behind the scenes

There is always a behind-the-scenes story of every publication, and lines of opportunity, serendipity, and curiosity that draw its authors in particular directions. This book has emerged from a collaborative venture between two authors, Dawn Mannay and Vicky Timperley (née Edwards). We both returned to education as mature students with children, and undertook undergraduate, postgraduate, and doctoral studies in the social sciences. We were (and still are) interested in qualitative research, creative methods, social justice, and contributing to informed policy and practice aimed at improving the experiences of the communities we engage with in our work. These overlaps in positionality, academic, and methodological activities and understandings of inequalities were a foundational connective base in our first collaborative project in the summer of 2013.

The 2013 study, titled *University Challenge*, explored the experiences of mature undergraduates in higher education. We produced data that was used to generate strategies to better support students, engendering some ongoing positive changes in practice in the sector (see Mannay and Edwards, 2015; Mannay and Ward, 2020). The study was also our first experience of using sand, together with objects and figures, in qualitative interviewing. Dawn had learned about the World Technique, which was developed by Margaret Lowenfeld (1939), who employed sand trays and figures as a form of child and adolescent therapy. We discussed Lowenfeld's work and thought about how it could be adapted from a therapeutic technique to a qualitative research method. This was the beginning of our journey with sandboxing.

Initially we created a homemade kit comprised of an old wooden drawer and play sand. We then added toys and other objects that we found around our homes. Following this initial project, we invested in a wider range of equipment and, with our shifting of the technique from psychoanalysis to qualitative research, we decided to name this adapted method 'sandboxing'. Over the past decade, we have drawn on sandboxing in further studies and seen it employed by other researchers. Accordingly, a diverse range of participants have engaged with sandboxing, including care-experienced children and young people, young parents, people with intellectual disabilities, children whose mothers are in prison, bereaved children, individuals who have experienced debt, children transitioning to secondary school, and young queer Latinx men.

We have published journal articles and chapters featuring reflections on sandboxing (see Mannay et al, 2017; 2018a; Mannay and Turney, 2020). However, there was no dedicated handbook available to support the growing interest in this method. This absence was brought to our attention by Dr Helen Kara, who invited us to contribute to the Creative Research Methods in Practice Policy Press series. The book series features short practical books by and for international researchers focussing on how to use different creative and innovative research methods. Therefore, we were pleased to be able to contribute to this series with *Sandboxing in Practice: Qualitative Interviewing with Sand, Objects, and Figures*.

Audiences and aims

The interest in creative research methods has grown in recent decades and this book is written for both those with experience of other techniques such as collage, drawing and LEGO® bricks, as well as individuals who are yet to engage with arts-based or multi-modal research. This is a book for researchers, but we take a wide view of this term. Consequently, we have written a handbook that will support full-time and part-time undergraduate and postgraduate students in the social sciences, health studies, human geography, social care and social work, and psychology who undertake studies in research methods and a research project as part of their studies. At the same time, we also kept in mind experienced academic and practice-based researchers, as well as other professionals who conduct or oversee research, and are considering adopting sandboxing in their future projects.

In thinking through our intended audience and what we wanted our book to offer readers, we decided that it would be useful to sandbox our ideas. As illustrated in Figure 1.1, we selected figures and objects to represent our ideas about creative research methods, sandboxing, and what we hoped the book would achieve. In the centre of the box is fencing, with a gap between the two sides illustrative of the collaborative nature of this writing venture, joining the figures on the left-hand side selected by Vicky with those on right-hand side chosen by Dawn.

Before reading our explanations of the sand scene in Figure 1.1, you may want to consider how you would have interpreted each object in the photograph and assigned meaning. In Chapter 3, we think through the juxtaposition between the audience's reading and the internal narrative of images, as intended by their creator; reflecting on auteur theory and its premise that the most salient aspect of what is created is what the maker intended to communicate (Rose, 2001). However, for now it might be interesting to experiment with your own assumptions and see to what extent they correspond with or differ from their creators' intentions.

For Vicky, the shape of the heart in the sand was traced as an expression of a genuine love for sandboxing as an approach and as her initial introduction to the world of creative research

Figure 1.1: Sandboxing this book

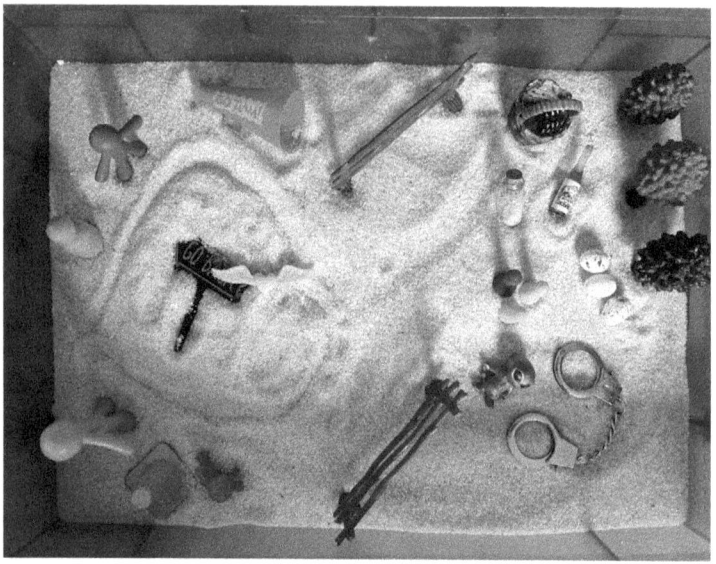

methodologies. Sandboxing was Vicky's first encounter with creative methods, and the 'go back' sign partially masked by sand symbolises the burial of the doubts and imposter syndrome that she experienced at that time as a working-class, mature student and mother in higher education. The sign 'go back' was annotated with a winged heart, which symbolises how sandboxing provided Vicky with the 'wings' and the confidence to become a creative researcher, taking flight on her own academic journey. The safety cone was added as a representation of how Vicky thought about sandboxing and about collaborating with Dawn, on starting the *University Challenge* project. The cone is a safety net, rather than a barrier, symbolising that Vicky was not alone but instead in a collegial, creative, and safe space.

This experience defined Vicky's commitment to creative techniques and continuing approach to qualitative research but her sand scene also reflects on other aspects of creative methods. For example, the collegiality of the creative methods community was centralised with the circle of figures. Vicky positioned these figures as lifting each other up and cheering each other on, and in our discussion, Vicky noted that not everyone in academia is fortunate enough to have this supportive circle of like-minded colleagues. The megaphone extends this conceptualisation of the cheering squad, emphasising the ways in which creative methods researchers amplify each other's contributions and share ideas. The invitation to join the creative methods community and experiment with sandboxing is the 'warm welcome' that we both wanted to extend to readers of this book, or in the Welsh language 'croeso cynnes'.

Dawn wanted this book to be a celebration of creative research methods, and sandboxing in particular, which was illustrated with the champagne bottle. The handcuffs are related not to incarceration but to the salience of links, so that the story of sandboxing is presented within the historical narratives and approaches that acted as a springboard to its use in qualitative inquiry. At the same time, the blue alien is a salient reminder of how unfamiliar ideas, terms, and concepts can be alienating. Therefore, it is important for the book to offer scaffolding to get people started, rather than using unexplained jargon and making assumptions about previous knowledge.

The trees and the eggs are the same category of object yet different in pigmentation and they were selected to indicate the flexibility of sandboxing and its adaptability to different participants, contexts, and research questions. The trees are also symbolic of sandboxing being rooted in Indigenous knowledges, therapeutic practice, and qualitative inquiry. At the same time, trees are always growing and branching in new directions and eggs hatch to reveal new forms of life. The basket is also very much about others taking the sandboxing method as part of their toolbox of creative methods, combining sandboxing with other techniques. For Dawn, the basket and eggs also resonated with the colloquial phrase 'don't put all your eggs in one basket', again emphasising the need to be open to opportunities to diversify. Dawn felt privileged to have seen colleagues and students work with sandboxing in new and exciting ways and positioned this book as an opportunity to share ongoing developments with sandboxing and to inspire others to continue to innovate and to improve sandboxing techniques.

The chess pieces were included as a reminder to be careful and considered in writing this book, doing justice to the approach, and to Helen Kara's Creative Research Methods in

Practice Policy Press series. Then there is the sand within the sand illustrated by the glass bottle filled with sand and corked to maintain separation. For Dawn, this held multiple meanings. The separation relates to the gap between what is placed in the tray and what is shared, and how the metaphoric quality of the apparatus means that participants can change their mind about the narrative of an object, having control over holding back, altering, or communicating the original meaning. This ambiguity is countered by the representation of grains of sand as grains of truth, and for Dawn the book needs to move beyond the partial truths of what went wrong and could have been better, with the researchers and authors, Dawn and Vicky, being prepared to be honest and critical of their own practice.

The book then aims to offer a detailed account of the 'how to' of sandboxing, thinking through equipment, practicalities, analysis, and adaptions so that the reader will feel more prepared to include sandboxing in their research. Additionally, it reflects on the philosophical underpinnings of creative and participatory approaches and how they relate to sandboxing. The sandboxing technique's links with therapeutic practice are also an important point of reflection as are the associated ethical considerations. The following section sets out in more detail the content that will enable the book to meet its aims.

Synopsis of each chapter

Each chapter of this book has been organised to lead the reader through what we feel are essential themes for gaining an understanding of sandboxing. Chapter 2, 'Sandboxing: from therapeutic practice to qualitative data generation', acknowledges the long history of sand and storytelling in Indigenous communities before documenting sand tray therapy and the World Technique, and examining the psychoanalytical traditions that underpin these therapeutic approaches. The chapter outlines how sandboxing is informed by therapeutic approaches, but also illustrates how it is distinct from this earlier work as a tool of qualitative research rather than a psychological intervention.

Chapter 2 also considers the move towards participatory and creative research approaches and the ways in which sandboxing aligns with these traditions. However, the chapter notes the ethical issues associated with transferring psychoanalytically informed tools into qualitative research practice (Frosh, 2010). Furthermore, it argues that sandboxing, like other creative methods, is not naturally or necessarily participatory, and that critical attention should be given to the framing of sandboxing in terms of the potentialities and limitations of collaboration and co-production.

Chapter 3, 'Sandboxing in practice', reflects on the use of objects in elicitation interviews more widely before showcasing a range of case studies featuring the use of sandboxing. Case studies with adult participants include sandboxing with mature students in higher education (Mannay et al, 2017), Queer Latinx men in Australia (Haro, 2022), people with intellectual disabilities (Mannion and the R&S (Relationships and Sexuality) Research Team, 2024), young parents (Mannay et al, 2018a), young people who have experienced debt (Coffey et al, 2023), and domestic abuse support workers (Maniatt, 2023). There is also a focus on engaging with care-experienced children (Mannay and Staples, 2019; Mannay et al, 2019b), children transitioning to secondary school (Turney, 2021), children whose mothers are in prison (Rees et al, 2017), and parentally bereaved children (Lytje and Holliday, 2022).

These case studies are introduced critically with a focus on both the limitations and affordances of the sandboxing method. The case studies focus on different aspects of the process; for example, sandboxing in action, analysing data, and researcher wellbeing. The case studies also attend to concrete questions about the benefits of sandboxing individually or collaboratively, how sandboxing works with other techniques of data production, the issue of negotiating ethics *in situ*, and what to do when participants do not want to work with sand and figures.

Having outlined some examples of the doing of sandboxing, Chapter 4, 'Sandboxing – adaptions and developments' considers extensions to the original sandboxing method. The chapter examines a range of adaptions, including the introduction of water to the sand tray (Watson et al, 2021), augmenting figures with craft materials (Turney, 2021), and using the sandboxing figures and objects in different contexts such as a doll's house (Mannay, 2019a). Chapter 4 also considers how sandboxing scenes and figures can assist researchers in disseminating findings and creating impact, while retaining anonymity for participants (Mannay, 2019b; Mannay et al, 2019b).

Chapter 5, 'Conclusion' draws together the key strands of the book and makes suggestions for future studies interested in adopting or adapting sandboxing, and for readers wanting to know more there will of course be a range of follow-up references cited throughout the book that can be explored to consider key points with more depth and complexity.

We hope that you will enjoy reading *Sandboxing in Practice: Qualitative Interviewing with Sand, Objects, and Figures*, and that it will support you to introduce this method or similar techniques in your own research. If you do decide to engage with the sandboxing method in your future projects, please do let us know about any unexpected outcomes or novel adaptions and updates that you introduce. We would be very happy to hear from you if you would like to share your sandboxing journey with us.

2

Sandboxing: from therapeutic practice to qualitative data generation

Chapter summary

This chapter begins by situating sandboxing within Indigenous practices of sand as a knowledge-producing and creating medium, rejecting the 'coloniality of design' that often silences the historical legacy of creativity outside of the geo-political North (Dahal and Gautam, 2024, p 25). It then introduces European psychoanalytical traditions and therapeutic approaches, and documents how material objects have been utilised to access the unconscious and support clients to make sense of traumatic experiences. There is an acknowledgement of the how sandpits have been used in play therapy, leading to an emphasis on sand trays in Margaret Lowenfeld's World Technique. The transference of the sand tray from therapeutic spaces to techniques of qualitative research is discussed as an introduction to sandboxing. The sandboxing method is then outlined, in terms of its equipment, and a case example of its first use in a research study briefly outlines the stages of data generation analysis. Lastly, critical attention is given to the associated ethical considerations and the extent to which sandboxing can be seen as a participatory approach in qualitative research.

Sand, yarns and Indigenous knowledges

Everyday creativity is 'latent in all communication and cognition' (Khoo, 2024, p 9) and creative practices in everyday life vary across contexts and cultures. Yet, despite its global presence and salience, academic interest in creativity is often overshadowed by Western world views that ignore local and Indigenous movement and methods (Dahal and Gautam, 2024). Nonetheless, Indigenous research pre-dates Euro-Western research by tens of thousands of years (Cram et al, 2013, p 11) and it encompasses a diverse range of approaches and frameworks (Kara et al, 2021). Accordingly, the communicative properties of sand that facilitated knowledge sharing amongst Australia's First Nations people originated long before the strands of European psychoanalysis outlined later in this chapter (Green, 2014).

Australian Indigenous academic Tyson Yunkaporta (2019, p 17) defines 'Sand Talk' as 'an Aboriginal custom of drawing images on the ground to convey knowledge'. Yunkaporta (2019) documents how attempts to share Indigenous knowledges with wider settler publics have been hampered by the tyranny of long-form written expression and concerns with objectivity. Sand Talk is a complex language, but its definitions are often over-simplified, relying on irrelevant and inaccurate categorisations of cultural knowledge. For example, to communicate an understanding of time, Yunkaporta provides an image that looks like a flower containing three concentric circles. The image, he explains, depicts the structure of family relations and the eternal cycle of time, wherein time and place (or space) are exactly the same thing. This is an Indigenous ancestral interpretation of the pattern of time in a cosmos where nothing new is ever created or destroyed, which is not easily understood by those who adopt more linear conceptions of time.

Sand Talk forms an integral part of a rich, interdependent, interpersonal oral culture, where symbols and images created in the sand convey the complexity of Indigenous thought and knowledge. Sand Talk often forms part of 'the generative cultural practice of yarning' (Yunkaporta, 2019, p 16). Sometimes over-simplified as storytelling, 'yarns' are a long-standing, traditional cultural form, the practice of conversing to generate and transmit knowledge. To some extent yarns are the earliest form of what we hope is achieved through the production of academic texts and evidence.

Recognising the need to translate Indigenous thinking and practice to forge connections beyond the communities employing them, Yunkaporta (2019) has been collecting yarns and stories since 2012. 'Umpan' is his method of translation, where Sand Talk and yarns are distilled into a simulacrum of a 'logic sequence' and carved into traditional objects such as shields or boomerang (Yunkaporta, 2019, p 16). Referred to throughout the writing process, these creations are the basis of Yunkaporta's translations. Distinguishing complex from complicated, Yunkaporta argues that it is the translation of visually represented, complex ideas into the representational form of the occupying power that is where the complications begin. For Yunkaporta, there is no place for shared, embodied knowing and contingent knowledge creation in an abstraction that freezes those things in time, a static quality that characterises the written, published form.

This book is of course in a written and published form, and we are not claiming equivalence with Sand Talk and yarns. Yet it has been important to begin with Indigenous approaches and briefly outline some key ideas. Yunkaporta (2019) critiques enlightenment-style thinking, synonymous with colonialist hierarchies of knowledge and its dogmatic adherence to logic, dialectics, objectivity, and empiricism. This book acknowledges this critique and Chapters 2 and 4 foreground the complexity of subjective knowledge that can be conveyed through sand and story wherever that takes place. However, the key influence on our development of the sandboxing technique came from psychoanalysis and therapeutic practice, and therefore the following section makes clear the associations and differences between this earlier therapeutic work and its later adaption for qualitative research.

Psychoanalysis and therapeutic practice

Creative and visual activities, including work with sand, have a central place in psychoanalysis and therapeutic practice. Material forms such as ink blots,[1] photographs, and drawings can be seen psychoanalytically as a route to the unconscious, with the meanings attached by the client, and shared through talking therapy, being projections of what was previously repressed. In a Freudian understanding, repression can be defined as an 'unconscious exclusion of memories, impulses, desires, and thoughts that are too difficult or unacceptable to deal with in consciousness' (Loewenthal, 2023, p 7).

Although Sigmund Freud is infamous for his psychosexual stages of development[2] from infancy to adolescence, these conceptual frameworks were mainly generated from the retrospective accounts of adults (Milton et al, 2011). Freud suggested that through play children could master the traumatic events that they encountered, but it is in the later work of Anna Freud that play is centralised, and toys and arts-based techniques become part of the therapeutic process. Anna Freud's approach reflected her father's adult psychoanalysis, in the extent to which she was interested in unconscious motivations, and she analysed the products of play in a similar process to dream analysis (Cattanach, 1992).

Klein's object relations approach departed theoretically from some Freudian thinking, yet her work was also psychoanalytically informed, with play furnishing direct access to the child's unconscious (Klein, 1975). In this way, Freud's ideas were developed, primarily by Melanie Klein, into a theory that regarded play as a symbolic representation of wishes, ideas, thoughts, and experiences (Davis, 1992).

The therapeutic affordances of play were also centralised by practitioners with an interest in techniques centralising non-directive play therapy. The work of Lowenfeld will be examined in the following section but it is worth noting here that her approach was both psychoanalytically informed and non-directive. Virginia Axline is renowned in this field, and her approach stresses the relational qualities in the interactions between child, therapist, and the materiality of play, and the ways in which the therapist needs to follow the child's interests and expressions rather than imposing their own perceptions and questions (Axline, 1947).

In non-directive play therapy, the child is accepted without any judgement from the therapist and there is no direct pressure to change, instead the child is seen as agentic and capable of solving their problems (Cattanach, 1992). Axline (1964) illustrates this approach in her book dedicated to the case study of one child, provided with the pseudonym Dibs, who was able to resolve significant issues through psychotherapy in the form of play therapy. The facilities for play were varied, including a dolls house, drawing materials and play figures. There was also a large sand pit, where Dibs could immerse himself in the sand, bury figures out of sight, build mounds, and introduce toy vehicles, soldiers, and doll's house figures to create stories. Dib's engagement with the sand is reflected in Axline's case notes of his associated talk.

> Bury things. Bury things. Bury things. Then dig them up again, if you feel like it … I tell you this sand is good stuff. (Axline, 1964, p 184)

These features have significant overlaps with the use of smaller sand trays and miniature figures, which as discussed in the following section are essential aspects of Lowenfeld's World Technique.

The World Technique

It has been beneficial to outline the Indigenous practices of sand and yarning (Yunkaporta, 2019) and to highlight how psychoanalysis and play therapy have contributed to the development of sand tray techniques. However, it was learning about of the World Technique that directly led to the development of the sandboxing technique. Accordingly, it is necessary to provide a clear overview of Margaret Lowenfeld's work to understand its influence on therapeutic practice, qualitative research, and sandboxing specifically.

Margaret Lowenfeld was born in 1890 to Henry nc Heinz Lowenfeld, a businessman of Polish Jewish origin, and Alice Evans, daughter of a Welsh naval captain from a non-conformist Protestant background (Unwin, 1988). Lowenfeld qualified from medical school in 1918, later specialising as a paediatrician, and her interests in child psychotherapy led to her establishing the 1928 Clinic for Nervous and Difficult Children, which later became the Institute of Child Psychology (Hutton, 2004).

Lowenfeld respected the work of key psychoanalysts and was influenced by Freudian approaches. Yet, while she undoubtedly made use of psychoanalytic theory, Lowenfeld did not wholly accept its principles as the foundation for her approach to child psychotherapy. Aligning with the position of Klein, Lowenfeld was concerned that Freud's theory of psychic development in the child illustrated an overreliance on the psychoanalysis of adults for its verification, rather than an investment in the first-hand accounts of children themselves (Davis, 1992).

Klein had already introduced toys into her practice, but she approached child therapy from a different theoretical and clinical orientation than Lowenfeld, who argued that the psychoanalysis of the 1920s and 1930s was too limited when applied to the play of children (Hutton, 2004). Lowenfeld argued that 'while … play of the kind described by the psychoanalytic school does certainly exist, this conception cannot be taken to cover more than a certain part of the total field of children's play' (1935 cited in Davis, 1992).

For Lowenfeld, psychoanalytic theory, at least as applied to the therapy of children, was something that needed further adaption and innovation. Lowenfeld did accept the importance of unconscious processes, but she found psychoanalytical practice far too restrictive, favouring a more holistic approach that recognised the strengths of the individual child (Unwin, 1988). Accordingly, Lowenfeld emphasised the importance of the child's discovery of their own meaning of their play (Hutton, 2004).

This focus on the child learning about themself in relation to the therapist aligns with the practice of non-directive play therapy discussed in the previous section (Cattanach, 1992). Lowenfeld afforded children the freedom to choose their play activities, and corresponding with Axline's (1947) approach, the therapist was positioned as a comrade or playmate during play, rather than an adult who should direct, correct, or criticise. Nonetheless, Lowenfeld recognised the unavoidable influence of the presence of the therapist, contending that children's play was only genuinely spontaneous when the child was free of the adult gaze (Davis, 1992).

It was important for Lowenfeld to find a technique to empirically address critiques that posited children's interior worlds as inaccessible. Freud had invested in tracing developmental forces back through adulthood, while Anna Freud and Klein had refocused the lens with their studies of children progressing through developmental stages. Lowenfeld was eager to move beyond theoretical conceptions and focus on empirically qualifying the usefulness of working with children. Aligning with the work of Piaget (Harris and Butterworth, 2002), Lowenfeld was also keen to design an approach that recognised the ways in which children think in a qualitatively different way to adults. Accordingly, she designed a multi-sensory instrument that could engage children, facilitate direct contact with their interior experiences, and be transparent and replicable for other psychoanalysts and practitioners in the field.

> A child does not think linearly as the adult is capable of doing; thought, feeling, concept, and memory are all inextricably interwoven. A child's thought is fluid, and movements can take place upon several planes at once. An apparatus therefore which will give a child power to express his ideas and feelings must be independent of skill and must be capable of the representation of thoughts simultaneously and in several planes at once, must allow of representation of movement and yet be sufficiently circumscribed to make a complete whole, must combine elements of touch and sensation as well as sight. (Lowenfeld, 1950, p 326)

The outcome of Lowenfeld's consideration of a suitable apparatus to meet these requirements led to her development of the World Technique. In terms of equipment, the Word Technique requires a stand and a container. Lowenfeld used a big metal tray, painted black outside and blue inside, set on a table of medium height. The tray would be filled with sand and Lowenfeld provided children with three types of sand: fine, coarse brown sand, and silver sand (Davis, 1992). Children could add water to the sand, making mouldable wet sand or simply keep the sand dry, or use a combination of both options. The tray could also be used empty of sand if children preferred not to work with sand.

For some children, water and sand were involved in children's play to the exclusion of any toys or objects. However, in her practice, Lowenfeld ensured that a cabinet would be placed beside the tray containing small objects representing things commonly found in a world; for example, houses, trees, people, both ordinary, military and fantasy, animals, wild and tame, transport of all sorts, trees, fences, lamp posts, and street signs (Lowenfeld, 1950).

When Lowenfeld delivered a presentation on the world pictures of children in 1938, she was criticised for the sense of constriction in the provision of a set apparatus, particularly by other therapists who placed importance on children finding objects, rather than being provided with objects (Davis, 1992). However, these critiques do not seem to fully acknowledge the affordances for imagination and creativity beyond the fixed equipment that was central to the World Technique.

For example, in addition to these toys and miniature figures, Lowenfeld also offered children a range of other art-based materials, including coloured paper, coloured and plain sticks, plasticine, and glitter (Lowenfeld, 1939). For Lowenfeld, ideally the presentation of the objects to children would be one in which all items were visible, rather than a design where children would need to open and close different drawers to access different elements of the equipment (Lowenfeld, 1950). While this does not afford opportunities for children to explore a jumble to find objects, there is a role for discovery in the bringing together of sand, water, objects, and art materials.

Lowenfeld invited children to make whatever they chose to create, without any adult intervention. For Lowenfeld (1939), this non-directive approach offered an opportunity for the child to be confronted by their own feeling, thinking, remembering as they constructed a world created by themselves for their own study. Lowenfeld used the term 'symbolization' to describe the means whereby a child might discover any aspect of experience contained in the inner world through their use of outside objects or materials like those provided in the World Technique apparatus (Davis, 1992). Accordingly, Lowenfeld maintained that the worlds created by children, with figures in the sand tray, were a projective tool enabling the expression of thoughts and feelings on a symbolic level, where the intricacies of the child's relational worlds could be transferred on to the material provided for play.

The children could offer a running commentary of the world that they created, which could be sufficient to scaffold the therapist's understanding. Alternatively, once finished, the child would be invited to explain the elements of their world. Lowenfeld advised that the therapist should not attempt to interpret the symbolism of the world but rather wait for the meanings to be identified by the child, 'in recognition of the multiplicity of meanings the world may contain' (Hutton, 2004, p 607). In this manner, the figures in the sand tray become a primary vehicle for intra-personal and interpersonal communication, where 'each figure holds unique and personal meaning for individuals' (Sangganjanavanich and Magnuson, 2011, p 266). Lowenfeld reflected on this uniqueness of meaning.

> Children use this apparatus in a very large number of different ways, and the main characteristic of their use, once the first strangeness of the material has worn off is unexpectedness. No object therefore, and no arrangement of objects, should be taken at face value, but careful inquiry made of the child as to what exactly each object in the world is to be recorded as being. It is essential for the proper understanding of the nature and use of this technique that no interpretation be given by the therapist to the child. (Lowenfeld, 1950, p 330)

The descriptions offered by children were recorded by means of a written description that included what the child had said, and also supported by drawings and diagrams. These records were used to gain an understanding of the interior lives of individual children, but Lowenfeld also recorded patterns across these records, noting recurring symbols and the mental conditions with which they correlated (Davis, 1992). Despite Lowenfeld's (1939) contention that it is important to centralise the subjective perspective of the participants, rather than applying the therapist's own interpretations and assumptions to their pictures, there was arguably a level of adult interpretation. For example, Davis (1992) notes that Lowenfeld's clinical records suggest that 'she and her co-workers did in fact interpret quite a lot along explanatory or educative lines'. Nonetheless, this form of explanatory analysis only took place after the child had first had the chance to describe what they had created, and it was centred on trying to understand the meanings and connections made by the child.

It is important to note that there was an expectation that children would be able to engage with the World Technique on more than one occasion. Lowenfeld (1950, p 331) argued that the first world created by the child could only provide insights into the most 'superficial layers of a child's thought'. Accordingly, the

World Technique, and the discussions that it evoked would be an ongoing therapeutic tool offered across play therapy sessions.

The World Technique was critiqued by Lowenfeld's contemporaries in the field of psychoanalysis for being restrictive, as noted earlier (Davis, 1992), and in relation to the ongoing debates related to conceptual frameworks of the unconscious and routes access to interior worlds (Hutton, 2004). However, Lowenfeld's Word Technique was appreciated by therapists, practitioners, and academics in the fields of psychology, medicine, and education, who had observed its benefits for children (Unwin, 1988). As documented in the following section, this appreciation led to developments and adaptions in Lowenfeld's techniques.

The World Technique – developments and adaptions

Lowenfeld developed a suite of instruments in addition to the World Technique and their value has been illustrated in their longevity. Yet, Lowenfeld's work has sometimes been overlooked, anonymously integrated, or misrepresented in later applications including tests of traits, temperament, and personality (Hutton, 2004). Lowenfeld was anxious that the World Technique should not be 'misunderstood or distorted when part of the equipment is borrowed and adapted for a different purpose' (Lowenfeld, 1950, p 325). Yet, at the same time, Lowenfeld was pleased for her foundational ideas to be applied in both different contexts and with modifications where this reworking was well considered.

Lowenfeld's friendship with the renowned anthropologist Margaret Mead was influential in her work being adapted as a tool for cross-cultural research (Unwin,1988). For example, Lowenfeld's Mosaic Test, which was a tool rather than a test, was designed to enable children and adults to explore and express their interior experiences, and to facilitate therapists' understanding and diagnosis of any problems. The tool consists of mosaic pieces that are laid out ready for use in a box, with which the individual makes shapes and later discusses them with the therapist. What was made and how it was assembled was intended to provide therapeutic insights into the child's or adult's view. However, following Mead's influence, Lowenfeld's Mosaic Test has been used by anthropologists in cultural and cross-cultural studies to examine participants' approaches to the world in different geographical contexts (Woodcock, 1984).

Mead also stimulated Lowenfeld's interest in educational research (Unwin, 1988). Lowenfeld invented the Poleidoblocs to portray basic mathematical relationships in a medium attractive to children. The Poleidoblocs consist of 54 wooden blocks, in primary colours shaped as cubes, cuboids, cylinders, triangular prisms, cones, and pyramids. The Poleidoblocs apparatus were designed for children to gain sensual and visual images of the mathematics behind the shape, and they are still used today to assist children in primary schools to discover mathematical concepts (Unwin, 1988). Accordingly, both the Mosaic Test and the Poleidoblocs apparatus moved beyond the confines of therapeutic practice into new fields, namely anthropology and education.

In terms of the World Technique, with the consent of Lowenfeld this was modified in 1956 by Dora Kalff, a prominent Jungian mentored by the influential Swiss psychiatrist and psychoanalyst C.G. Jung Carl. Kalff used the same equipment, a box filled with sand and miniature figures, but coined the term Sandplay to differentiate her approach from Lowenfeld's (Lytje and Holliday, 2022). Sandplay is now a term that is restricted for use by clinicians who are trained in Kalff's Jungian-based approach (Sangganjanavanich and Magnuson, 2011). Following her Jungian traditions, Kalff used Sandplay as a projective technique and felt that it enabled clients to 'go beyond the limits of the conscious mind, to stimulate psychic development and to access channels to fuller, more creative living' (Turner, 2023, n.p.)[3]. As with the World Technique, there is a wide body of practice-based case study evidence in a variety of contexts that has supported the therapeutic value of Sandplay (Pearson and Wilson, 2019).

Although Lowenfeld was the originator of the apparatus, arguably Lowenfeld's work has become less well known than that of Kalff in contemporary applications of Sandplay (Hutton, 2004). However, while the term Sandplay is firmly located in Jungian practice, the use of sand trays and the term sand tray is a more generic descriptor that can be applied to any therapeutic use of the equipment originally designed by Lowenfeld (Sangganjanavanich and Magnuson, 2011). There have also been named adaptions including 'expressive sandwork' used in group settings without the framework of psychotherapy; an informal style of play therapy, similar to Axline's case of Dibs introduced earlier in this chapter, termed 'sand tray work'; and the self-discovery expressive therapies style of sand play that integrates Kalff's methods and principles within a creative arts context (see Pearson and Wilson, 2019). Sandboxing can also be seen as an adaption of the World Technique, but as will be discussed in the following section, this is an adaption that shifts the apparatus from the domain of therapy to a method of inquiry in qualitative research.

From therapy to qualitative research

As with the earlier adaptions, sandboxing began with an introduction to the work of Margaret Lowenfeld and, in particular, the World Technique. Dawn attended an annual conference organised by the British Psychological Society in April 2013, where one of the sessions focused on the therapeutic benefits of work with sand and figures. Dawn had worked with creative methods of data production including drawing, photographs, and collage in earlier studies (Mannay, 2010; 2013) and was about to undertake a new project where she felt that the materials used in sand tray therapy may be useful tools of data generation.

As discussed in Chapter 1, Dawn and Vicky worked together on the study, titled *University Challenge*, which explored the experiences of mature undergraduates in higher education. Vicky researched the literature around sand tray approaches, and we found Lowenfeld's approach a useful foundational base that we could adapt for use as a tool of qualitative data generation. Lowenfeld's approach was non-directive with the child seen as agentic and capable of solving their problems (Cattanach, 1992), and we also positioned participants as agentic and capable of telling their own stories and directing the research conversation. For Lowenfeld, it was important that the meanings of the sand scene should be identified by the child, rather than the therapist attempting to interpret the symbolism of their miniaturised worlds. Again, this aligned with our approach to analysing visual materials, privileging the premise of auteur theory, where the most salient aspect of what is created is what the maker intended to communicate (Rose,

2001). As will be discussed in the following sections, there was a clear distinction between Lowenfeld's therapeutic practice and our role as qualitative researchers; nonetheless, we were able to draw relevant lessons from the World Technique for our work with sandboxing.

The *University Challenge* project did not have any funds to purchase a manufactured sand tray kit so our initial challenge was to create apparatus that would enable our participants to create a sand story of their experiences in university. Vicky was able to get help to upcycle an old wooden cupboard drawer into a sand tray, and we purchased children's play sand. The next step was to bring together a wide enough selection of miniature objects and figures to enable a choice of metaphorical[4] and literal materials for participants' stories. We also wanted to follow Lowenfeld's model of offering things commonly found in the world such as houses, trees, people, animals, transport, trees, fences, and street signs (Lowenfeld, 1950).

With this in mind, we went in search in our homes to find items and make a list, and in writing this book and returning to our Word documents from 2013, we called these lists an 'inventory of sand box objects'. The formality of our document titles is perhaps illustrative of our commitment at the time to trying to do this in the 'right' way. Vicky had a child at home young enough to play with toys, and as illustrated in Table 2.1, she searched for items that remained faithful to Lowenfeld's key categories. Vicky was also careful to adhere to Lowenfeld's advice that the category of people should contain fantasy figures such as Tinkerbell, a pirate, witches, and wizards, as well as military figures, with the inclusion of a soldier. There were also the recommended materials to divide and demarcate within the sandbox, such as fences and rocks, which were well utilised by participants in the study.

Dawn's children were way past the toy stage in 2013, and she did not have the same access to the defined category resources, and instead collated the items listed in Table 2.2. These may appear to be a random assortment of items, and Dawn felt that their contribution was not really hitting the Lowenfeld criteria, except maybe in the miscellaneous category. However, in collating the items there was a consideration of the potential metaphorical meanings that some objects could hold for a mature student,

Table 2.1: Inventory of sand box objects – Vicky

Animals	People	Landscape	Transport	Miscellaneous
Pig ×3	Gatekeeper soldier	Wooden fencing ×5	Ambulance	Marble
Large dinosaur	LEGO® men ×2	Grey boulders ×3	Motorbike	Green felt
Small dinosaur	Man – menacing look	Beige rocks ×5	Red bus	Fabric bowl
Spiky dinosaur	Androgynous PLAYMOBIL®	Greenhouse	Campervan	Wooden block
Tropical bird	'First people' warrior	Traffic cones ×4	Orange car	Orange pegs ×2
Wooden frog	Postman	Toadstools	Yellow car	Pebble
Turtle	Woman figure	'Do not enter' sign	Green jeep	Lolly sticks ×17
Fluffy chicks ×4	Woman farmer	Small building	Helicopter	
Dragon	Girl dressed as a witch	Assorted trees ×9	Taxi	
Dragonfly	Witch	Rope ladder	Train	
Ceramic snail	Wizard	Stairs	F1 racing car	
Ladybird	Tinkerbell figure	Row of plants	Dumper truck	
Tiger	Pirate	Clock tower	Aeroplane	
Dog ×3	Father Christmas			
Goat ×3	Fighting soldiers ×3			
Horse ×5	Spaceman			
Bull ×5	Taekwondo action figure			
Cat ×5	Woman builder			
Sheep ×2	Scarecrow			
Rabbits ×3	Man figure – shirt and trousers			
Cow ×8				
Chimp				
Lizard				
Goose				
Elephant				
Lion				
Chicken ×2				

Table 2.2: Inventory of sand box objects – Dawn

Frog eraser	Homme Dior sample	Five pence	Conker	Flower brooch
Mole ornament	J'adore Dior sample	Two pence	Coal	Flower ring
White sheep	New Zealand pin badge	One penny	Fossil	Flower jewel
Brown horse	Manchester United pin	Large grey button	Shells ×4	Daffodil badge
White horse	London Olympics badge	Small black button	Safety pin	Pewter heart
Miniature masks ×2	Cardiff University badge	Small tartan button	Plectrum	Silver heart
Candle	Cancer research badge	Small glass button	Screw	Purple heart
Battery	Welsh rugby pin badge	Arabic bead	Golf tee	Blue heart
SIM card	Star pin badge ×2	Paper clip	Key	Marble heart
Drawing pin	Smiley face ball	Giant paper clip	Football	

with Dawn reflecting on her own experiences of university in the process of object gathering. In our meeting to sandbox the book, as outlined in Chapter 1, there were discussions of our first sandboxing endeavours. Vicky had remembered the paperclips in Table 2.2, reflecting that in 2013 when she asked the question, 'what are they for', Dawn's reply was that 'paperclips hold things together'. The idea that something will fall away can be a concern for mature students with often competing demands of caring responsibilities, employment, and study (Morgan, 2016). Therefore, what may appear meaningless can generate poignant metaphoric engagements and these items were drawn on by participants to convey a range of experiences, hopes, and fears.

It is important to note that the materials offered to participants in this study differed from the apparatus provided to children as part of the World Technique in two distinct ways. As discussed earlier in the chapter, alongside the sand and figures, Lowenfeld (1939) supplied art-based materials, including coloured paper, coloured and plain sticks, plasticine, and glitter. Additionally, in Lowenfeld's approach children could add water to the sand (Davis, 1992), changing its texture and form and enabling more definition in structuring the landscape of the sand scene. In this study there was no provision of water or any of these art-based supplies.

As we will discuss in Chapter 4, both water and crafting equipment can bring affordances to sandboxing in research studies (Watson et al, 2021; Staples et al, 2024). Therefore, when reflecting on this early study Dawn wondered, with a sense of contrition, if we had missed an opportunity, and whether we should have introduced these options to participants. However, Vicky remembered this exclusion differently, recalling that after having to put everything together with no funds to purchase extra equipment, and only having one sandboxing kit, we did not want our sand to get mixed up with glitter and plasticine, or to be left with wet sand that would not dry in time for the next interview. We had no direct experience of undertaking this approach before; but as parents we were accustomed to the loss of individual colours in mixed-together plasticine, the results of outside sandboxes with lids forgotten and exposed to rain, and the implausible infiltration qualities of small pots of glitter. This is an important point because as much as we wanted our research designs to offer choice, variety, and the conditions for creativity, we also need to keep in mind what was practical and possible within the time and financial resource of our project.

Once we had brought together our equipment, it was offered to participants in the study, mature students (n = 9) that had undertaken or enrolled on a social science degree programme at a university in Wales. The students constituted three groups: participants that had completed their undergraduate degree programme (n = 3), participants that had completed their first year (n = 3), and participants due to enrol in the following academic year who were in a preparatory program (n = 3) (see Mannay and Edwards, 2015).

Participants were seen on an individual, rather than a group, basis and, for participants who had undertaken university studies, the scenes created represented the experience of their first year as an undergraduate. Students who had not yet begun undergraduate level study created a sand scene focused on their expectations, hopes, and fears around embarking on a trajectory in higher education. Participants were then asked to describe their sand scenes in audio recorded interviews and the sand scenes were photographed so that they could support the analysis of the interview data.

Data were analysed using an inductive and deductive approach, creating overarching thematic categories and analytical themes arising from coding and categories across the data sets. The findings were written, outputs were generated, and given the barriers faced by mature students reported here and in previous studies (Busher and James, 2018; Morgan, 2016), the evidence base was drawn on to enable concrete support systems to be put in place for mature and non-traditional students (Mannay and Ward, 2020).

This is an intentionally brief overview of how we initially adapted Lowenfeld's World Technique to a tool of qualitative inquiry. In Chapter 3 there will be a dedicated focus on the nuances of working with sandboxing in terms of data generation and analysis, and its affordances, limitations, and practicalities. Accordingly, the next chapter will be very much about the 'doing' of sandboxing; but before that, a question that we need to attend to is one that asks if ethically speaking we should be 'doing' sandboxing at all.

Sandboxing – objections and ethics

There have been strong objections to qualitative researchers utilising equipment or frameworks that originated in therapeutic practice as tools of data generation with participants. For example, there have been accusations that it is unethical to take psychoanalysis outside of the clinical situation of the consulting room by importing its artefacts into the research arena (Frosh and Emerson, 2005; Frosh, 2010). An example of this is the reaction by some scholars to the qualitative interviewing technique developed by Wendy Hollway and Tony Jefferson (2000), the Free Association Narrative Interview (FANI). Therefore, it is useful to engage with this earlier borrowing from psychoanalytical practice that has responded to these criticisms, to inform an evaluation of the ethics of sandboxing.

Central to the use of the FANI is the idea of a 'defended rather than unitary, rational subject' or more simply put: participants, and all people in a general sense, have a dynamic unconscious that defends against anxiety (Hollway and Jefferson, 2009, p 296). People, as defended subjects, use defences such as repression so that unhappy memories will not come into consciousness. The FANI technique elicits free association to try and gain an insight into these defended aspects of the human psyche, those aspects that people have hidden even from themselves.

The ideas of an unconscious, repression and free association are drawn from the psychoanalytical work of Sigmund Freud. For Freud, the domain of the human mind that is not ordinarily accessible is divided into the unconscious proper and the repressed unconscious. The unconscious proper has always been inaccessible, and no one knows what it contains. The repressed unconscious holds what was once conscious, and therefore knowable and known, but has been pushed into the unconscious. For Freud, these repressed thoughts and memories can still be accessed through dreams, neurotic symptoms, and free association (Milton et al, 2011); and he paid close attention to these three access points in his psychoanalysis of patients.

Freud claimed the status of natural science and made careful case notes of his patients talk and other cues through empirical observations (Midgey, 2006, p 215). However, while his foundational work is still drawn on in psychoanalysis and other psychotherapies, his methods and conceptual frames have been critiqued as 'non-scientific' in the field of psychology and social science more generally. Psychoanalysis has an ambiguous status in mainstream research and has become what Parker (1998) terms psychology's repressed other. Even contemporary approaches, such as psychoanalytically informed psychosocial inquiry are often excluded or ignored in handbooks of qualitative psychology and social research methods (Mannay, 2013; Folkes, 2015). Accordingly, Hollway and Jefferson were entering difficult territory by drawing on Freud to inform their approach; but they were clear that their work is psychosocial research and not psychoanalysis.

> A psychosocial approach to empirical research is not psychoanalysis, rather it means, in my practice, critically using psychoanalytic ideas, both ontologically

and epistemologically to 'fill' the empty subject of discursive psychology in productive, if inevitably provisional, ways. (Hollway, 2011, p 238)

In their psychosocial work they are interested in understanding participants as constructed in particular social, cultural, and historical contexts, appreciating the 'social' within the psychosocial. However, there is an influence of both sociological and psychoanalytic traditions, and for Hollway and Jefferson there is an emphasis on the importance of conflict and the unconscious. In terms of data generation, their FANI approach aligns with qualitative interviewing, offering participants an opportunity for a largely uninterrupted flow of talk with an attentive listener whose role it is to try and understand what is being said. Their framework of analysis considers social and cultural norms, local cultural practices, and the biographical narratives of participants; areas of focus that align with mainstream qualitative inquiry. Yet, in the analysis of the data, particular attention is also given to instances of incoherence, contradiction, and avoidance, which are seen as potential sites of free association that can offer differential insights.

There is not room to delve into this work in any depth in this book and the best way to understand this approach is to read papers where it is applied to interviews with participants. The detail and complexity in this work often necessitates a focus on one participant in published works, and the term 'case' is employed, again borrowed from therapeutic practice. In our teaching of third-year undergraduate students, we have introduced this psychosocial approach through cases, and we would recommend 'the case of Ivy' (Hollway and Jefferson, 2001), 'the case of Vince' (Hollway and Jefferson, 2005a), and the relevant critiques and rejoinders (Hollway and Jefferson, 2005b; Wetherell, 2005) to those interested to learn more.

For now, it is worth noting that this approach does have supporters, and it has been argued that psychoanalytically informed psychosocial research addresses subjectivity in a more nuanced way than mainstream psychology (Clarke and Hoggett, 2009). There is then some agreement that we 'need to understand human subjects as simultaneously the products of their own unique psychic worlds and shared social worlds' (Gadd and Jefferson, 2007, p 4). Yet, tensions remain about whether it is ethical to use any concepts that originated with Freud given the controversies around his work, as well as questions about whether techniques central in therapeutic practice should be used by researchers who are not trained therapists.

The work of Lowenfeld has not been subject to the same criticisms directed at Freud. However, the FANI approach is psychoanalytically informed rather than psychoanalytical or therapeutic, and we would position sandboxing in the same way. Sandboxing as a methodological tool is an adaption of Lowenfeld's World Technique, but as with the other uses of Lowenfeld's apparatus in the fields of education and anthropology, we are not using this apparatus for therapeutic practice. Nonetheless, we appreciate that there are ethical concerns with sandboxing that are similar to the those levied against research using creative methods more widely. Sandboxing does not risk anonymity in the same way as studies using photograph or film (see Clark, 2020; von Benzon, 2024) but, like other creative data-gathering techniques, sandboxing can be a 'sharp tool' (Burnard, 2018).

Participants' involvement with approaches like sandboxing can engender more emotive and emotional engagements because of its mnemonic qualities and the time and space it affords for reflection and reflexivity (Kara et al, 2021). Additionally, as participants select the objects to build their worlds and lead the conversation, the accompanying interviews may move beyond the intended topic and take both participants and researchers on unintended and unexpected journeys. We will embed discussions of ethics and ethical practice in Chapter 3, but it is worth noting here that it is not the techniques themselves that are inherently good, and ethical approval does not always necessitate ethical research. For Loewenthal (2023, p 134) 'appropriate thoughtful practice can be more ethical than an ethical code'. Therefore, although institutional or organisational codes provide a starting point, with sandboxing, as with all tools of data-gathering, we need to think about situated ethics and the ongoing responsibilities of researchers to have the best interests of participants at the heart of their projects (Renold et al, 2011).

Naturally or necessarily participatory

In addition to queries about the ethics of the origins of sandboxing, another frequent question we are asked is the extent to which sandboxing is participatory. The simple answer to this question is that no tool of data generation is inherently participatory, so it depends how sandboxing is used and how participatory practice is understood.

Participatory approaches are aligned with research that is 'with' participants, rather than 'on' research subjects. The researcher then is positioned as a participatory facilitator, enabling participants to lead and direct elements of the research process (Pauwels, 2011). Questions of 'how participatory' a study is are often focused on which elements of a study participants are invited to lead, coproduce, and collaborate on and where their active participation is excluded, rather than encouraged. A holistically participatory study would involve participants from the design of a study through to stages of data generation, analysis, and dissemination. Yet, for the majority of studies participation is concentrated in the data generation phase with little opportunity for participants to contribute more widely, situating the approach as 'partially participatory' (Mannay, 2016, p 12).

The extent to which studies are participatory has been explored in early models, such as the 'Ladder of Participation' (Hart, 1992, p 8) and adaptions of this model (Reddy and Ratna, 2002). More recently, scholars have drawn on the philosophy of Reggio Emilia to explore the extent to which studies are and can be participatory (Chicken et al, 2024). Questions around participatory practice are also linked with approaches advocating for 'voice' – this has sometimes been referred to as giving 'voice' – but participants already have a voice of their own, and a participatory methodology cannot simply 'give voice' to participants (see Lomax, 2012; Chadwick, 2021).

There is an expectation that sandboxing itself is participatory and this is in part because of the easy marriage between visual and creative data production and participatory practice. Historically, visual artefacts and creative forms such as crafting have been employed as a vehicle for marginalised and politically oppressed communities to challenge the status quo and record their stories through cloth work, photography, and painting (Bacic, 2013; McEwan, 2003). However, these examples are grass-roots movements and forms of 'individualised political activism demonstrating flexible and decentralised networked forms', which should not be confused with the more formalised methods of social research (Mannay, 2016, p 6).

Therefore, just because a method is creative, it should not be assumed that it is participatory. As will be illustrated in Chapter 3, sandboxing can provide opportunities for participants to metaphorically build worlds, and lead conversations that communicate the complexities of their experiences. Accordingly, the sandboxing technique has participatory potential, and it can feature in research designs that seek to incorporate elements of participatory practice, but sandboxing is not inherently, naturally, intrinsically, or necessarily participatory.

Conclusion

This chapter has offered the reader a story of the journey to sandboxing both in terms of the roots of the approach that have branched to new adaptions, and the personal journey of the authors in developing this as a tool of data generation. The chapter began with a consideration of sand stories and Indigenous practice. This was an important starting place because as Kara (2024a, p 59) contends, 'Indigenous researchers have known for millennia what Euro-Western researchers are groping towards (and still, in some cases doggedly rejecting): story is research; research is story'. Accordingly, it was useful to consider how sand has been used as a tool to document both mundane and complex messages, and to convey stories effectively to others, long before it became popular in European psychoanalysis and therapeutic practice.

Therapeutic practice was then outlined with reference to the psychoanalytical work of Sigmund Freud, Anna Freud, Melanie Klein, and Virginia Axline. This overview set out a foreground to the work of Margaret Lowenfeld, and there was an emphasis on the World Technique. The chapter then documented how the authors of this book, Dawn and Vicky adapted Lowenfeld's World Technique from a psychoanalytical therapeutic intervention to a tool of creative data production, 'sandboxing', with reference to their first collaborative study incorporating sand and miniature figures. Lastly, as we are often asked about both the ethics and participatory potential of sandboxing, we outlined some key points of response.

This chapter was written to provide an overview of the earlier work that influenced the development of the sandboxing technique, an insight into how it was first applied in practice, and a sense of some underlying ethical tensions and misrepresentations. Chapter 3 will work with a range of case examples to illustrate how sandboxing has been used to attend to diverse research questions, in different settings, with various modes of data production and frameworks of data analysis.

3

Sandboxing in practice

Chapter summary

This chapter is concerned with how sandboxing has been adopted as the basis for interviews in qualitative research studies. It begins by outlining a range of case examples from studies over the past decade that illustrate the affordances, limitations, and ethical considerations of working with objects, figures, and sand. It then introduces studies that have combined sandboxing with other creative techniques of data generation, including body mapping, collage, diaries, drawing, and timelines; exploring the interactions between these different methods and the layering of insights into participants' lives and experiences. Data analysis is an aspect of research that often 'receives the least thoughtful discussion in the literature' (Thorne, 2000, p 69); therefore, the chapter also outlines some frameworks that have been applied to make sense of the data generated in studies using sandboxing. Before concluding, the chapter offers some reflections on researcher wellbeing, as while ethical protocols and situated ethics prioritise the protection of participants, the emotional impacts that researchers negotiate are not always given significant attention.

Interviewing with sand, objects, and figures

Chapter 2 began with an acknowledgement of 'Sand Talk' as an Indigenous practice (Yunkaporta, 2019) and centralised the influence of psychoanalysis and in particular Margaret Lowenfeld's (1950) World Technique. However, the use of objects as tools of data generation more widely has also been a key consideration in our development of the sandboxing technique. Therefore, before discussing work with sand, it is worth noting that objects and figures have been utilised in a range of qualitative interview studies without the involvement of a single grain of sand.

For example, Rachel Hurdley (2006) conducted interviews with participants in Wales who were invited to tell stories about the origin and meaning of objects on mantelpieces and other display areas in their homes. This proved an effective approach to explore the ways in which the 'apparently 'private' experiences of the self are manifested by means of display objects and domestic artefacts' (Hurdley, 2006, p 717). Again, in the space of the home, Grant et al (2018) asked new mothers in Wales to share objects that represented their infant feeding practices. They noted that participants were enabled to direct conversations around their objects with the 'interviewer taking the position of actively listening to the accounts of participants', rather than simply raising a series of interview schedule questions to be answered (Grant et al, 2018, p 435). Nonetheless, the researchers found that in a case where the participant did not bring any objects, they initially found it more difficult to facilitate the flow of conversation. This acts as a salient reminder of the importance of being well prepared for occasions where participants may not want to engage in object-based research methods.

As well as participants discussing their own possessions in research studies, objects can be offered by the researcher. This approach was taken by Constantino Dumangane Jr. (2016), who employed objects as a mechanism to encourage young adult participants to feel more comfortable about sharing their personal journeys of being Black African Caribbean undergraduate students in elite UK universities. The objects were a set of cufflinks that he had collected, and participants were asked to select cufflinks to represent their relationship with their mother, father, caregiver, or a significant person in their life, and then discuss the reasons that they chose specific cufflinks. For Dumangane (2022), this object-based method enabled him to break out of the prescribed question–and–answer directive, which can be a constraint of qualitative interviewing. Additionally, the cufflinks aided participants in 'describing and constructing their lived experiences' and in imagining their relationships through objects (Dumangane, 2022, p 9).

There are then alignments with the use of objects, without sand, and the participant-led conversations that were featured in these studies reflect a key affordance that we aim to facilitate with sandboxing interviews. However, the introduction of the sand tray in combination with objects and figures can offer a more embodied and multi-sensual experience for participants. This was a feature of the *University Challenge* project (Mannay and Edwards, 2015), which we outlined in Chapter 2, as in addition to telling their stories about being mature non-traditional students in Wales, participants worked actively with the sand to communicate movement, change, and pressure.

In the elicitation interviews around their sand scenes, participants discussed feeling isolated within the academy, and many articulated the problematic nature of balancing family commitments and work; forming a support network was often difficult. In constructing representations of these experiences in their sand trays, participants did not always simply select objects and place them statically on the sand, rather the sand formed part of their stories. This is illustrated by a partially buried Tinkerbell (see Figure 4.4 in Chapter 4) whose immersion in the sand was an important part of the of the participant's representation of her experience as a mature student.

> I partially buried her because she's like in quick sand, because there's too much for one person to do … she can't do it all, but she has to do it all so she has to keep her body out and she's like flailing her arms, but you can't really, so you're sort of half, you're always half sunk but you're trying to carry on. (Mannay et al, 2017, p 353)

Accordingly, we can position the sand as active in this process (Taguchi, 2011), because it enables the figures and objects to be completely or partially buried. There were also instances of movement. For example, one participant set out a scene within the sandbox (Figure 3.1) and then enacted a series of movements within the elicitation interview to illustrate how they saw

Figure 3.1: Confronting barriers

themselves overcoming barriers in their education trajectory (Figure 3.2). This illustrates the fluidity of the sandboxing materials to support participants to communicate their experiences.

In the interview, the participant moved the figures in the sand around a mound that they placed above the level of the rest of the sand. In their accompanying narrative they explained how they had considered withdrawing from their studies because of barriers they faced within and beyond the institution; but later they became determined to complete their studies to improve the lives of their own children.

> I just thought, that's it now, there's no way I'll give up, I'll finish it and I'll get a first and (laughs) and that's what I thought, so I thought, you know, I'll smash, you know, I'll knock that bloody 'Do Not Enter Down', I'll knock all them out and then I'll slay the class dragon and then that was sort of, you know, bring it on, so I thought, yeah, after that lecture when I walked out I thought there's no way that I will leave now. (Mannay, 2019a, p 327)

Figure 3.2: 'Slay the class dragon'

This element of movement, and also submerging figures in the sand, was a feature of participants' engagement with sandboxing in Rhiannon Maniatt's study examining the ways in which workers supporting women in Wales who have experienced domestic abuse can be impacted by vicarious trauma. It is worth noting that not all participants in this study wanted to engage with sandboxing because they felt more comfortable with the alternative option of a qualitative interview without this activity. As one participant commented, 'I think if there's a thing in my head, I have the best chance of conveying it to your head with my words' (Maniatt, forthcoming), while one participant who was familiar with the therapeutic use of sand trays felt that engaging with the sand and figures would be too emotive given the vicarious trauma they had experienced in their role. These accounts highlight the importance of providing participants with alternative ways to engage in research, a shared feature of all the studies outlined in this section.

However, some participants preferred to 'show' as well as 'tell', and Figure 3.3 illustrates a participant's sand scene depicting a

Figure 3.3: Positive aspects (reproduced with permission from Rhiannon Maniatt)

Figure 3.4: 'Swamped' by work (reproduced with permission from Rhiannon Maniatt)

family, friendship, and other aspects of their lives that they feel are positive. In contrast, Figure 3.4 is the participant's representation of being 'swamped' by work and the sand has been swept across so that the avatars representing family are submerged and the avatar of the participant is face down in the sand (Maniatt, forthcoming).

This movement then is important for participants communicating stories in the sand tray, but in their research with queer Latinx men in Australia, Adriana Haro (2022) also reported movement with the figures and objects even before they entered the sand tray. In this study, participants engaged with a series of interview questions prior to the sandboxing activity, but the figures and objects were set up in advance and close to hand, and some participants chose to engage with them throughout their interviews.

> Another participant played with the figures and held the stop sign figure throughout most of our interview. He was having a conversation with me, however having the miniature figures nearby seemed like it made the interview process less awkward for the participant. (Haro, 2022, p 107)

This tactile engagement with the figures through sensation seemed to act as a source of comfort, illustrating the potential of the method to facilitate self-soothing; examples of such self-soothing are evident in other studies. For example, research conducted by Martin Lytje and Carol Holliday (2022) invited a sample of bereaved Danish children aged between 4 and 8 years to create sand scenes representing their memories of when their parent had been ill or died. Given the nature of the study, the child's surviving parent was present and there were other measures including each session beginning with everyone sitting together and sharing a meal, the child being provided with the choice of telling their own story or one of a fictional child or friend, and careful closure protocols. The authors found that the sand tray acted as a safe space for children to recount their memories, and they reported that 'some children would allow the sand to flow through their fingers during difficult parts of the conversation' as a method of self-soothing (Lytje and Holliday, 2022, n.p.). Despite the sensitivity of the topic and the relatively young age of the participants, Lytje and Holliday (2022, n.p.) contend that their careful application of the technique created 'an environment where the participant and researcher can explore sensitive matters safely and positively'.

Procedural ethics are essential in ensuring that researchers carefully contemplate the potential risks, 'but they are not sufficient on their own, and it is thereby vital that researchers consider the wider implications and the need to behave ethically 'in the moment" (Ellis et al, 2023, n.p.). This careful work was evident in the Lytje and Holliday (2022) study with bereaved children and attention to ethical practice was also a guiding principle in a sandboxing study with care-experienced children and young people. This Welsh Government commissioned study was designed to explore the educational experiences, attainment, and aspirations of care-experienced children and young people in Wales (Mannay et al, 2015; 2019b).

Social care and legal processes involved in placing a child or young person into public care involve social work encounters, which have alignments with interviewing. Therefore, it was important to move away from question-and-answer style interview techniques and offer participants different ways to engage. We met children and young people in all-day events with a range of different activities available such as T-shirt printing, clay modelling, bag making, and jewellery design, which were not part of the data generation design. If children and young people wanted to be involved in the research element, we invited them to create miniature worlds with sandboxing equipment that either reflected on their educational experiences or their aspirations for the future, which were discussed in individual elicitation interviews.

The examples of sandboxing discussed in this section have focused on participants creating sand scenes, but in this study researchers also created representations of their experiences. It is essential to acknowledge the positionality of researchers within processes of data generation, and this joint sandboxing approach was adopted so that children could ask researchers questions about the contents of their sand scenes, rather than the researchers gaining insights into participants' lives without offering to share their own experiences (Mannay et al, 2015). This process of communal engagement enabled children and young people to find out more about the researchers in a bidirectional process through the sharing of reflections and future-orientated aspirations.

It is important to note that none of the children and young people demonstrated any observable distress when discussing their sand scenes, even when their accounts touched on their separation from parents and siblings, or their hopes for different circumstances in the future. While these may be perceived as traumatic or emotional events, this perhaps is 'testament to the resilience of care-experienced children and young people, or reflects a weary familiarity with sharing details about their personal lives with non-familiar adults' (Mannay et al, 2017, p 354).

There was an instance of the disclosure of a potential safeguarding issue following work with sandboxing; however, the research team were able and willing to effectively deal with disclosures. Furthermore, arguments against engaging children and young people on an affective level in research, through creative techniques like sandboxing, for fear of this occurring, is unsatisfactory, as attending to disclosures can potentially contribute to an improvement in participants' safety and well-being (Mannay et al, 2017). Overall, the sandboxing activities fostered valuable opportunities for children and young people to have their feelings acknowledged and heard in a safe space.

This section has discussed the usefulness of objects in qualitative research and emphasised how the addition of sand can enable further opportunities for expression as participants can bury objects and figures, change the contours of the sand tray landscape, and act out scenes. It has also as reflected on how figures and objects can act as a source of comfort during interviews and how working with sand can facilitate self-soothing. There was also an acknowledgement of some of the ethical considerations for working with sandboxing, and the importance of ensuring participant well being and safeguarding in the design of sandboxing studies. The following section will introduce studies that have worked with sandboxing in combination with other techniques and consider how this multi-method approach has the potential to generate more nuanced understandings of participants' lived experiences.

Sandboxing with other techniques

Researchers often draw on different techniques of data generation within their research studies. This use of multiple approaches can be a way of gaining insights into different aspects of participants' lives and experiences, with participants engaging with a range of techniques in the same research sessions or in repeat or longitudinal research designs. Offering a combination of ways to engage in research can also be a strategy to ensure that participants have some level of choice about how they engage in research, and in some studies, participants and collaborators are involved in the design stages, selecting the research tools that will be provided in the main study. This section will outline sandboxing studies that incorporate other methods for these reasons.

In the opening section of this chapter, Grant and colleagues' (2018) study where new mothers in Wales shared objects that represented their infant feeding practices was introduced. The open nature of the object elicitation process meant that participants not only brought objects related to infant feeding but also shared objects representing wider aspects of parenthood, health behaviours, and representations of how they felt that the pregnant body was policed. These findings led us, the researchers, to apply for funding for a further three studies that explored issues that were important to the new mothers in the original study (Mannay et al, 2018a; 2018b; Grant et al, 2019; 2020), one of which offered the option of sandboxing.

The study worked with ten mothers who were less than 30 weeks pregnant in their initial interview, followed by an interview conducted before the birth of their child (Mannay et al, 2018a). Before engaging in an initial interview, participants were invited to create a timeline that facilitated a life history interview (Berends, 2011; Adriansen, 2012; Mannay and Creaghan, 2016), which seven of the mothers completed. Prior to the second interview, mothers were sent a collage kit, which four completed, and a word bubble activity, which six completed to represent their feelings around their pregnancy. They could engage with one, both, or none of these pre-tasks depending on their own personal preferences.

During the second interview, participants discussed their collage and word bubble activity, if completed, and nine women engaged with a sandboxing exercise to metaphorically illustrate the impact of pregnancy on their everyday lives. In the sandboxing activity, the shared experience of motherhood was used to facilitate discussion around these topics. The researchers were either pregnant, or already had children, and both researcher and participant built a sand scene of their pregnancy. As in the shared sandboxing activity with care-experienced children and young people (Mannay et al, 2015), this meant that participant and researcher could share aspects of their lives with each other. The interview around the sand scenes in this study became a discussion between two women about their differential understandings of the shared experiences of pregnancy.

Many participants found the joint sandboxing activity more engaging and accessible with the researcher working alongside them on their sand scene. The shared element of the sandboxing alleviated the previous concerns that participants had about producing the 'right' sort of collage or word bubble, and having a working example *in situ* increased their confidence to engage. While instructions were posted out with the other activities, these were not as informative or as reassuring as creating something side by side.

While the collage and word bubble added elements to the interview discussions, the combination of the timeline and sandboxing activity were the most effective techniques for understanding participants' accounts of their pregnancy and, where they had older children, their maternal relationships. For example, one participant used the figure of a lion in their sand scene to illustrate her need to protect her children from the outside world. This metaphor was related to her 'biographic account of being bullied at school and her fears for her children's future' (Mannay et al, 2018a, p 771).

One participant engaged in discussing the researcher's sand scene but found it difficult to construct their own sand scene. They did not place any figures or objects within their sand tray but instead used the sand as a medium to write the word 'complete'. This could be seen as a form of disengagement but in relation to the biographical details that were shared in the earlier discussion of the participants' timeline, this single word was a poignant representation of what motherhood meant to the participant. As Eldén (2012, p 76) contends, creative productions are 'part of the whole picture and cannot be separated from the talk' and in this study the elicitation interviews were important, but the text of the timelines offered biographical details that contextualised participants' meaning-making in the later activities.

Exploring issues around mothering from a different perspective, an evaluation of the Visiting Mum scheme was conducted by

Alyson Rees and colleagues (2017). The Visiting Mum scheme was a three-year project that worked with Welsh female prisoners, housed in English prisons, because there are no women's prisons in Wales. The scheme facilitated contact between mothers and their children during the period of the women's incarceration. As part of their evaluation, the research team interviewed women and prison staff, conducted a survey with staff in related organisations, and also consulted 12 children at the prison to gain their views and experiences of the Visiting Mum scheme.

Before working with the children, the research team observed a Family Fun Day organised for a large group of children to visit their mothers, where a range of activities were undertaken with children and young people. The later research reflected this element of diversity in the options that children and young people could engage with, and they were invited to complete a timeline collage, create a sand scene representing visiting their mother in prison, and to draw eco maps. This research design aimed to facilitate involvement, aligning with the Mosaic Approach (Clark and Moss, 2001), which has been evidenced to generate more participatory practice because of its focus on a choice of tools of data generation and its recognition of children and young people as competent and active subjects, capable of providing information about themselves.

An elicitation approach was taken, and the research team talked to children and young people as they created their representations, as well as organising focus groups or individual interviews around key themes based on the preferences of the participants. The combination of techniques worked effectively to enable children and young people to share different aspects of their experiences and as illustrated in Figure 3.5, the sandboxing activities offered an opportunity for participants to represent how they felt about Visiting Mum scheme visits compared to the ordinary prison visits.

> This is just like an 'ordinary' visit (on the right). The big orange thing in this corner is the guard, he's watching over you like a control. The pterodactyl just feels like you're always being watched and if you see the like in the corner that's just us three all close together because we can't really move around in here, we're stuck in one corner. And then all the people that are,

Figure 3.5: Comparing visiting provision (reproduced with permission from Alyson Rees)

all these little figures that are looking at us are because there's just so many people around and you always feel like you're being watched by everybody. And the spider represents as well like you don't feel as safe as you would with a PACT visit. (Rees et al, 2017, p 33)

In describing their sand scene, the young person explained what the objects and figures represented. The placement of figures and spacing between them also signified an integral part of their experiences, and the line in the sand demarcated the two types of visits. In this way, sandboxing enabled a space for reflection where children and young people could create and communicate their lived experiences, which were layered with their responses to the other activities to offer more nuanced insights. The qualitative interview with mothers and prison staff and the survey data were also beneficial in providing different perspectives on the Visiting Mum scheme.

In Australia, Julia Coffey and colleagues worked with 24 participants aged between 18 and 29 years old to explore the impacts of consumer credit debt on well-being through the use of qualitative interview methods alongside bodymapping and sandboxing. In bodymapping, a full-sized outline of a human body on paper is given to participants for them to annotate using words and pictures in repose to a research prompt. In this study, following initial interviews, participants were offered hypothetical scenarios based on themes from the interviews, which they responded to with bodymapping. Participants created a fictional person in the outline of a human body and were asked how they would pay for a costly car repair, or a large dental bill, and a desired designer pair of jeans. This technique of data production was adopted to explore how participants imagined debt and the 'embodied wellbeing impacts associated with debt and stress' (Coffey et al, 2023, p 690). Participants also engaged with sandboxing to reflect on and represent their own experiences of debt and the researchers found that the construction of sand scenes was useful for expanding the discussion about experiences of debt. For Coffey et al (2023, p 690), the miniature figures and objects were an effective means of accessing 'abstract aspects of experience, including the subjective and affective dimensions of wellbeing'.

The Coffey et al (2023) study illustrates how different techniques of data production can be applied to attend to different aspects of a study's central research questions. This was also a factor in Catt Turney's (2021) research, which explored how Welsh children imagine, narrate, and navigate their transitions from primary to secondary school. This study had a longitudinal design, which involved meeting the children four times between July 2016 and September 2017 and engaging them with a range of creative qualitative methods to explore school transition, its meaning, and how it was negotiated over time.

In stage one, children were asked to write their responses to the questions, 'What do you like about school?' and 'What do you not like about school?', and then to draw their response to the question 'What will it be like at high school?' within two separate thought bubbles, one with a smiley face for positive imaginings and one with a sad face where children could draw what they were concerned about in transitioning to secondary school. In this stage, and the following stages, the activities were followed by an elicitation interview.

Stage one generated a baseline of data about how children experienced primary school and how they envisaged the outcome of their transition to the next stage of education. These activities were reflected on in stage two, where children had experienced six weeks in secondary school and were asked to compare their pre-secondary school imaginings with their actual experiences, and to consider if the things they liked and did not like about primary school transferred across to the secondary school context. Children were also asked to create a paper timeline of a school day, using emotion stickers to indicate how they felt at different points. Emotion stickers have been an effective element of previous studies (Gabb and Fink, 2015; Mannay et al, 2018a), and use of emotion stickers in combination with timelines in this study 'aimed to explore participants' affective responses or attachments to parts of the school day' (Turney, 2021, p 73).

In this second stage, and the following stages, a set of plasticine was made available during interviews. Participants could use the plasticine to respond to interview questions; however, the children generally used this creative outlet to make models that were unrelated to their interview accounts. This form of playfulness was noted earlier in the chapter in relation to Adriana Haro's study where participants played with the sandboxing objects and figures, even when not engaged in creating their sand scenes. The plasticine was also used to augment sandboxing figures, which will be discussed in more detail in Chapter 4 and illustrated in Figure 4.3.

Stage three of the study explored the social aspect of transition through sandboxing in response to the prompt, 'tell me about important people in your school life' (Turney, 2021, p 73). In comparison to the drawing method in stage one, participants reported that they were less anxious about producing something 'good', which can be related to both the transient nature of sand scenes and the lack of any requirement for artistic skills. However, this was not a joint sandboxing activity as the researcher did not engage in tandem, and some children struggled with whether or not they were doing it 'right' and needed some assurance.

Children had completed a year of secondary school at stage four of the project and having become familiar with the researcher, and with some creative methods of data production, they were asked to reflect on key moments across the school year by constructing a paper timeline using drawing, collage, or writing, or using their choice of a variety of craft materials provided. The participants' parents were also interviewed in stage one and again in this final stage to provide an alternative view on the transition process. In all of the research encounters, the researcher focused on working 'towards making the research encounter a space in which the participants were listened to, supported and respected, and where discomfort was recognised and accepted' (Turney, 2021, p 82). This position recognised that some elements of transition, and their communication through creative modes of engagement, could elicit negative emotions but that these should be negotiated with an ethic of care, rather than being avoided, dismissed, or remaining unacknowledged.

The study was carefully designed with methods selected to explore different aspects of the transition. However, participants retained an element of choice in terms of how they wanted to respond, with the envisaged technique sometimes rejected with an alternative way of working adopted by participants to communicate their experience. There was also a participatory focus in the elicitation interview, where children directed talk and tangents were welcomed rather than a strict adherence to the focus of research questions. Yet, Turney (2021, p 84) warns against romanticising these freedoms as 'children participating in the project resisted and exercised power in ways that were not always easy to negotiate and sometimes had a significant impact on the project'.

A further difficulty in providing choice to participants is the transportation of materials. Turney (2021) had to travel on public transport, with lengthy walks to the research sites, carrying a significant amount of equipment. Paper, pens, plasticine, and arts materials are relatively lightweight but sandboxing figures combined with the sand itself contribute to a heavy load. The weight of sand has been problematic in conducting our own research and workshop activities. This was particularly noticeable in our initial sandboxing study (Mannay and Edwards, 2015) with a sturdy and weighty wooden box. In later sandboxing activities this was replaced with lightweight sand trays, yet the sand remained an issue when having to carry the equipment, particularly when more than one sand tray was required.

In writing this book, we have become aware of an alternative to sand that is significantly lighter and more portable. Helen Kara ran a creative methods workshop in May 2024, and in this session shared the issues Dawn had raised in 2020 when invited to bring sandboxing materials to a conference event, requesting that the organisers buy sand for the planned sandboxing activities. Attending the 2024 workshop with Helen Kara was psychologist Stephen Robinson who helpfully offered the advice that paper-based cat litter is much lighter and also sand-coloured (Kara, 2024b). This is something that we are yet to try, but we will certainly invest in this alternative and it is something readers may want to consider, particularly in projects that intend to combine sandboxing with other creative techniques of data generation.

This section has documented the usefulness of combining different methods to attend to different research questions. Catt Turney's work and other examples in this section have also illustrated participatory potential in relation to the choice and freedom offered to participants, and the opportunities to select their preferred methods of engagement and direct the associated conversations. However, as noted in the introduction to this section, participants can also be involved in the design of studies using multiple research techniques. A best-practice example of this collaborative approach is demonstrated in the work of Jess Mannion and the R&S (Relationships and Sexuality) Research Team (2024); however, as this involvement was from design through to dissemination, this study will be outlined in the following section, which has an emphasis on data analysis.

Analysing sandboxing data

As Kara et al (2021, p 84) note, analytic work should include 'meticulous preparation and coding of data, accurate description and representation' and it is important to consider the steps of analysis that have been adopted in work with sandboxing. The studies discussed in this chapter have all featured elicitation interviews where participants have explained their sand scenes. This approach aligns with the premise of auteur theory, which regards the most salient aspect of an image as what its maker intended to communicate (Rose, 2001; Mannay, 2010). Although it is not a therapeutic intervention or a form of psychoanalysis, sandboxing also reflects the therapeutic use of sand and objects documented in Chapter 2, where the psychotherapist does not 'seek to ascribe meaning but to explore with the patient' (Jayne et al, 2024, p 280). Therefore, the use of elicitation interviews around the sand scenes centralises the meaning-making and interpretations of participants, the creators of the sand scenes. In this way, the sand scene is the basis for a conversation where interpretation needs to be embedded in the contextualised process of the interview.

This approach recognises that sand scenes are imbued with meanings that could be misinterpreted, and therefore privileges the interpretation of participants as the first point of reference for data analysis. In this way the sand scenes and their discussion act as a 'bridge between people' (Harper, 2023, p 98), with participant and researcher in a communicative exchange that fosters understanding *in situ*. However, this is only the beginning of the analysis process as researchers need to examine the sand scenes and their accompanying interview audios and transcripts, and any field notes and reflections within the wider context of the field of research and relevant conceptual frameworks (Gauntlett and Holzwarth, 2006; Guillemin and Drew, 2010). It is also important to consider that in the same way that conversations *in situ* become abstracted typed transcripts, sand scenes, unless the process is filmed, can only be retained as two-dimensional photographs, which researchers need to reflect on in the analytic process (Rose, 2016).

In the sandboxing studies that we have conducted, the sandboxing activities acted as tools of elicitation rather than objects of analysis per se. However, we considered photographs of the sand trays and notes about the process in the analysis to clarify and extend the associated interview transcripts. These reflections on the process of data generation are important as analysis begins before what we may consider as the formal stages of interrogating a data set. For example, in considering interactions between individuals, Broomfield (2024, p 405) 'marvelled at the nature of the mutuality that exists beyond words'; and the movement of figures and objects in the sand trays, as well as the emotional resonances, both observed and felt (Mannay, 2018), can translate into touchstones of significance that inform the analysis of data.

In these sandboxing studies, we transcribed all of the interview data verbatim and analysed the transcripts alongside the sand tray photographs. We applied a thematic framework inductively, allowing codes, categories, and themes to be constructed from the data and also deductively, actively searching for themes that had been identified during our funding bids and reviews of the literature. Accordingly, our analysis was both grounded in the existing empirical and conceptual knowledge base as well as being an exploratory quest to extend the work of previous scholars and consider how any novel findings could be applied to policy and practice.

We undertook forms of thematic analysis that involved data familiarisation, systematic data coding, generating, and developing, reviewing, and naming themes (see Braun and Clarke, 2006; 2021). In the majority of these studies, this analysis was undertaken manually, on printed transcripts using colour coding and annotations by hand, or on a computer using multiple Word documents, again using colour and comments to sort and code the data set and develop key themes. In one of these studies (Grant et al, 2020), transcripts were imported into the Computer Assisted Qualitative Data Analysis (CAQDAS) tool NVivo 11 to assist with the coding process. CAQDAS programs do not analyse data for researchers, rather they provide a platform to store and sort data. However, the development of CAQDAS has enabled the inclusion of image-based data, which can be useful to 'identify broken links in thinking' between different modes of data (Silver et al, 2024, p 41).

In the Grant et al (2020) study, during both the stages of data production and analysis, regular meetings were held between all four researchers to discuss key threads, continuities, and contradictions. This sharing of ideas and reflections is a supportive mechanism within the data analysis process and one that has been adapted to different extents in our other sandboxing projects. These benefits of co-production were demonstrated in Jess Mannion's (2023) doctoral study where she devised a creative approach to analysis in collaboration with a group of co-inquirers with intellectual disabilities.

The co-inquirers working with Mannion selected research topics to explore and chose a range of techniques of creative data production, including sandboxing, and it was important that they were also involved in making sense of the data. The multi-stage co-analysis was designed to maximise accessibility and included visual interpretation, member checking, and content, art-based, and embodied forms of analysis, ensuring that co-inquirers were meaningfully engaged across the study (see Mannion and the R&S (Relationships and Sexuality) Research Team, 2024). As this example illustrates, analysis can be a collaborative process and can involve different approaches to analysis than the thematic approach that we have generally applied in our studies.

It is worth emphasising that there are not specific forms of analysis that are particular to sandboxing; rather, the techniques of analysis that can be used are varied and transferable from contexts where different methods of data production have been applied. Given that there is accompanying text – the participant's account of their sand tray – there are many options that can be drawn from studies with an emphasis on talk-based data. For example, following interviews with participants, Nelson-Miles (2024, p 71) felt that her data 'represented more than words to be coded, analysed and fitted into a thematic box'. Therefore, she took a narrative approach and developed micro-stories to represent the participants' key experiences. Sandboxing discussions could potentially be translated into micro-stories as part of the analysis process. However, rather than dismissing thematic analysis, it should be acknowledged that hybrid approaches like 'thematic narrative analysis' have identified themes within 'narrative analysis to explore the sequential organisation of events in participants' accounts' (Braun and Clarke, 2021, p 338).

Accordingly, there are a whole range of approaches that can be taken to analyse images of sandboxing scenes and their accompanying interview transcripts. These could include writing reflexive accounts in poetic forms (Dodding and Partington, 2024; John, 2024), translating data into a graphic novella (Carruthers Thomas, 2024), making an evidence wall of key visual and textual material (Gray and Lazenby, 2024), using the lenses of both discourse analysis and content analysis (Morgan et al, 2024) or creating word clouds to provide a structural and strategic means of eliciting and comparing the stories within the data (Gascoine et al, 2024). These forms of analysis can be drawn on at different stages of the research process and are not restricted to an end point of data saturation; and this ongoing back and forth between the generation of data and generating understandings of the data can be a worthwhile process with moments of serendipity, reconceptualisation, and revision.

Unfortunately, there are no 'data analysis fairies' we can call on to organise our data into 'a coherent new structure' that will explain everything (Thorne, 2000, p 69). However, undertaking analysis, although challenging is at the same time rewarding, and there are books that offer reflexive accounts of the 'how' of data analysis. Kara et al's (2024) edited handbook of creative data analysis would be one source that you could consider in thinking through both how to analyse creative data and how to analyse data creatively. As well as considering how to analyse data, it is also important to contemplate the potential impacts of analysis, as well as data production, on the researcher, which will be the focus of the following section.

Sandboxing and researcher wellbeing

'Emotion is not an intrusion into the research process, but a constitutive element of it' (Loughran and Mannay, 2018, p 2), yet the idea that researchers are an incidental inconvenience to the generation of universally valid data continues to overshadow ideas about what constitutes 'respectable' research. Within the social sciences and humanities over the past three decades the 'cultural turn', 'emotional turn', and the 'turn to subjectivity' have meant that relationality and researcher experience have garnered more academic attention and generated more nuanced understandings of the positionality of the researcher (Loughran and Mannay, 2018). Nonetheless, this has not necessarily extended to an interest in and attention to the wellbeing of researchers at all stages of the research process.

Researchers exploring sensitive topics will enter into the research process with some knowledge of the type of experiences participants may present, and an appreciation of the associated risks of harm to both participants and to themselves. Yet, in qualitative research, where participants can direct the conversation beyond the intended topic, and in arts-based or visual research projects participants may create materials 'representing feelings and ideas that defy or reach beyond participant and researcher vocabulary' (von Benzon, 2024, p 47). Therefore, creative methodologies, such as sandboxing, may take both the researcher and participant on unexpected journeys. For participants, there should be safeguarding and support mechanisms built into the study for it to gain ethical approval; but this does not assist the researcher.

In the fields of therapy, social work, and advocacy support there have been attention to the impacts of listening to traumatic accounts and its association with vicarious trauma. There has been a recognition that vicarious trauma is 'pervasive, that is, potentially affecting all realms of the therapist's life; cumulative, in that each client's story can reinforce the therapist's gradually changing schemas, and likely permanent, even if worked through completely' (McCann and Pearlman, 1990, p 136). Psychotherapists, social workers, and advocates will have clinical supervisions or other organisational mechanisms that offer opportunities to reflect on complex cases and discuss their wellbeing (Jayne et al, 2024; Maniatt, forthcoming). However, there are not always such supportive processes in place for researchers.

Bloor and colleagues (2010) conducted an inquiry into the physical and emotional harm suffered by qualitative social researchers and found that junior researchers and doctoral students were the main recipients of reported harms. Principal investigators have a responsibility for the wellbeing of their research teams, and doctoral supervisors should be cognisant of not just academic progression but also the mental health of their students. Nonetheless, respondents in Bloor and colleagues' (2010, p 45) study felt that they were being 'let down by some principal investigators and PhD supervisors who are failing to manage researcher risks effectively'. There has been a wider focus on wellbeing following this inquiry but the impacts of research on the researcher should not be underestimated.

The weight of emotional and cognitive impacts for researchers is poignantly communicated by psychotherapist Nicki Power who notes how in undertaking a literature review for a piece of research as a researcher, rather than working directly with clients as a therapist, she was 'saturated by the pain held in the stories of people' (Jayne et al, 2024). Accordingly, researchers can be impacted through reviewing the existing literature (Sheppard, 2018), in the process of generating data (Mannay, 2018; Roberts, 2018), in the close work of data analysis where they read, re-read, code, and interpret patterns (Grant, 2018), and in presenting research findings (Carroll, 2018):

> The stress points are particular to an individual and are not always visible to those around. A person may appear to be complete and be invisibly crumbling. (Treloar, 2015, p 79)

Therefore, it is important to have an awareness of our own emotional wellbeing and those around us, asking ourselves and our peers how they are negotiating the challenges of their research. Of course, this is not exclusive to researchers engaged in studies that involve sandboxing, but we did not want to write a guide that neglected this important aspect of undertaking research. There is a responsibility held by supervisors, principal investigators, and senior researchers to provide support but there are also alternative sources of support. For example, Agata Lisiak and Łukasz Krzyżowski (2018, p 33) discuss how face-to-face and virtual interactions with colleagues in the same research team can form integral support systems for researchers, which can help them negotiate 'both the emotionality of social-science research and the wider emotional labour of academic work'.

As well as supportive interactions within research teams, communities of practice with those working within the same field or methodological specialism can also act as a protective factor to mitigate the impacts of vicarious trauma and help with wellbeing (Jayne et al, 2024; Leigh et al, 2024). Using a research diary and engaging with other forms of reflexive writing can also help to process traumatic accounts shared by participants and difficult research encounters in the field (John, 2024). Creative methods are often presented as fun, and of course they can be, but, just like other qualitative methods, sandboxing can generate unexpected, unintended, and upsetting stories. Therefore, as well as forward planning to ensure the wellbeing of participants, researchers also need to build in self-care and support systems for themselves. For as a participant in the Bloor et al (2010, p 53) inquiry commented, 'If you haven't prepared for the worst, you'll be up the creek when it happens'.

Conclusion

This chapter has offered insights into work with objects and discussed how objects and figures can be combined with sand to enable participants to construct stories of their experiences and share them in elicitation interviews. It has also provided examples of the ways in which sandboxing can be combined with other qualitative methods of data generation, as well as outlining some ideas for analysing the data generated in studies involving sandboxing. The chapter has emphasised how generating and analysing data can be emotionally challenging, and the importance of considering the different ways that researchers can be supported. Accordingly, the chapter has provided a foundation for readers to consider the practical and ethical aspects of working with sand, objects, and figures alongside their accompanying elicitation interviews, which will prove useful for those wanting to incorporate sandboxing in their own qualitative research studies. However, there is still more to discover about sandboxing in terms of the adaptions and developments that researchers have made in their practice, which could provide further information and inspiration, and this will be the focus of the following chapter.

4

Sandboxing: adaptions and developments

Chapter summary

As Kara (2024a, p 59) contends, 'trying to pin down the methods of any one type of research is a necessarily doomed endeavour because people are endlessly, joyfully creative with research methods'. Accordingly, it is important to offer insights into these forms of creativity, and this chapter examines adaptions to the sandboxing method at different stages of the research process. The chapter begins by considering the data generation stage, focusing on the introduction of water to the sand tray, the use of the sandboxing figures in different contexts such as a doll's house, and how sandboxing figures can be modified with other materials. The chapter then reflects on the opportunities for sandboxing scenes and figures to act as tools of engagement in the dissemination of findings and in increasing impact while at the same time retaining anonymity for participants.

Sand meets water

Chapter 2 introduced Margaret Lowenfeld's World Technique, noting that in this therapeutic intervention children could choose to add water to the dry sand to make mouldable wet sand, simply keep the sand dry, combine both options, or they could use an empty tray if they preferred not to work with sand. In Lowenfeld's work, some children involved water and sand in their play without any toys or objects, while others introduced miniature figures to their sand trays. In our original sandboxing adaption (Mannay and Edwards, 2015), we did not offer an option of water, for the practical reasons outlined in Chapter 2. However, other researchers who have since adopted and adapted sandboxing have successfully incorporated water in their studies with children, young people, and adults, which will be the focus of this section.

Debbie Watson, Eleanor Staples, and Katie Riches worked together on the *Difficult Conversations* project. The project aimed to develop research-led training resources to support responses to care-experienced and adopted children's difficult life-story questions. Watson and colleagues wanted to find a creative method that provided participants with a non-threatening, safe space to discuss experiences, emotions, and memories that were often traumatic or ambivalent. For adoptive parents, foster carers, social workers, and children and young people who were care-experienced, difficult care conversations 'were both consciously and unconsciously threaded through their daily lives' (Staples et al, 2024, p 46). Therefore, the research team felt that it was important to select a method of data generation that could offer opportunities for participants to render this familiarity strange (Delamont and Atkinson, 1995; Mannay, 2010; Morriss, 2016).

The research team were aware of the development of sandboxing and its differentiation from the World Technique (Watson et al, 2021). They were also cognisant of how sandboxing had been used in previous studies with children and young people who were care-experienced; particularly as Eleanor Staples had also worked on these earlier sandboxing projects (Mannay et al, 2017; Mannay and Staples, 2019). Watson and colleagues (2021) were also drawn to Margaret Lowenfeld's premise that the World Technique was 'created by the children themselves' (Lowenfeld, 1979, p 281) when a set of toys, a tray, and some sand and water were made available for patients in her clinic. The team were interested in the role that water played when children combined this with sand and figures to create small worlds and sand scenes, which offered insights into their 'interior' selves (Lowenfeld, 1979).

The *Difficult Conversations* project involved interviews with a range of participants in England to explore the ways in which care-experienced and adopted children and young people have, or would like to have, conversations about their care journeys with professionals, adoptive parents, and carers. The project involved 11 children and young people who were adopted children (n = 5), an older adoptee (n = 1), and care leavers aged 18–20 (n = 5) (Watson et al, 2021). These children and young people were invited to engage in sandboxing to create a scene representing their hopes and fears about 'difficult conversations', which they then discussed in an elicitation interview. The team also conducted interviews with adoptive parents (n = 4), foster carers (n = 2), and social workers (n = 11) (Staples et al, 2024). These participants were asked to create sandboxing scenes representing their hopes and fears about having difficult life-story conversations with the child or children that they cared for, had adopted, or worked with in their social care role.

As in earlier 'sandboxing' studies, participants were each provided with a small portable tray filled with sand, and a selection of small objects such as vehicles, shells, animals, buildings, people, flowers, and trees. In addition to this standard equipment, each participant was provided with water in a jug for the creation of pools or to make the sand more buildable (Staples et al, 2024).

Despite some wariness about sandboxing, all of the participants who engaged in the activity later reflected that the method had been helpful because it enabled the time, space, and the 'physical material (of the sand and figures) to 'think things through' before being interviewed' (Staples et al, 2024, p 46). This space to think and reflect was also reported in relation to the studies presented in Chapter 3. Similarly, the use of metaphor with the objects and the incorporation of lines in the sand and gates to demarcate space were also salient aspects of the studies discussed in the previous chapter and the *Difficult Conversations* project. However, as illustrated in Figure 4.1 and the associated text from a participant, Sarah, the addition of water enabled participants to divide their sand scenes more clearly and to work with the sand itself as an effective building material.

> That's no man's land, that's where I am. This side is my family life, it's very hectic, it's a war zone, there's crumbling – no stability in the buildings, […] and the grass is always greener on the other side, this was my foster placement with, you know, big house, full of love

all the time but I still don't feel like I fit in anywhere. You know, all the bad side, there's nowhere for me, I just sit on my own little island in the middle [...] I came from poor upbringing with you know, abusive environment [...] and it was always very hectic and I went into a placement with this massive house with very tight family connections, you know, dinner round the table [...] and it wasn't really spoke about – about the fact that going from somewhere where you have nothing and being shown all these things that you technically could have had, it's kind of like, well, you know – [...] it's hard – I feel like it's something not really spoke about. (Sarah, 20 cited in Watson et al, 2021, p 669)

Figure 4.1 illustrates how Sarah was able to create her 'no man's land'. It also poignantly represents how Sarah built and partially destroyed the visualisation of her home of origin to communicate a sense of 'crumbling – no stability in the buildings'. Furthermore, the combination of sand and water enabled Sarah to create the

Figure 4.1: 'No man's land' (reproduced with permission from Debbie Watson)

scale and design of the foster family's 'big house'. The objects and figures still have their use within this sand scene, with the soldiers emphasising the idea of the 'war zone' and the hearts connecting with a house 'full of love'. Yet, this example from Sarah provides a compelling case for the affordances of including water so that the sand itself can be more malleable to support the building of participants' subjective understandings of their worlds. The building of forms that resemble traditional sandcastles in Figure 4.1 may also be a touchstone of acquaintance for participants who have experienced days at the beach, perhaps making sandboxing more familiar and less of an unknown for participants.

Accordingly, the addition of water to sandboxing activities is an important consideration for researchers. The therapeutic usefulness of water with sand has been demonstrated by the work of Margaret Lowenfeld (1979, p 6), whose conditions for the World Technique state that 'there must be an ample supply of sand and water, so that the maker may model any type of contour, and place objects anywhere in or on this sandy base'. Additionally, its benefits as a technique of qualitative data generation are evident in the *Difficult Conversations* project (Watson et al, 2021; Staples et al, 2024).

Nevertheless, as documented in Chapter 2, there are practicalities to consider. For example, whether researchers would be left with wet sand that would not dry in time for the next interview. This would mean replacing the sand each time so that every participant would have the option of wet or dry sand, which could be fairly inexpensive with standard play pit sand but not with the more costly glittery smooth sand that is available with some sand tray kits. Decisions about whether to incorporate water then will depend on the research topic, availability of materials, cost and sustainability, any restrictions in the venues used for data production, and a range of other factors unique to each study. The design of the study may also consider the place of the sand itself, which is the focus of the following section.

Figures outside the box

As discussed in Chapter 2, the sandbox has been a useful tool in therapeutic work as it enables children to bury objects and metaphorically communicate aspects of their lives in this active placement of miniature figures beneath the sand (Axline, 1964). In Chapter 3, the affordances of sand were illustrated across a number of studies, and they were also a feature of the sand and water examples introduced in the previous section. For example, there were key advantages in relation to participants being able to bury objects, as well as dividing the sand to demarcate areas and raise areas of the sand scene to symbolise aspects of their experiences. However, there are opportunities to use miniature figures within different structural backdrops, and the sandboxing kit figures have travelled to different settings, drawing inspiration from other studies using objects.

For example, Amie Hodges worked with young children who had siblings with cystic fibrosis, inviting then to draw pictures, create collages, and use their own toys and objects to communicate their experiences (Hodges, 2016; 2018). The artworks and material objects introduced by the children in the study formed the basis of elicitation interviews, where children shared their ideas about the actual or metaphorical meanings of their creations and everyday playthings. A participant in Hodges' study introduced their doll's house and dolls to discuss their everyday routines with different dolls representing family members and the rooms in the doll's house aligning with rooms in the family home. This was used to both re-enact family activities surrounding cystic fibrosis treatment and to communicate elements of fantasy about the life that the participant would have liked to live, poignantly expressed within the world of the doll's house (Mannay and Hodges, 2020).

This structure enabled by the architecture of a building, rather than a tray filled with sand, was incorporated in Dawn's study exploring young people's engagement with museums (Mannay, 2019c). The three-storey doll's house had been resident in Dawn's house along with an array of other toys that were play opportunities for Dawn's grandchildren and other child visitors. In thinking through museum spaces as containers for heritage, Dawn decided to offer the sandboxing figures and objects to participants with the doll's house rather than the sand trays that would usually accompany these figures and objects.

In the study, young people interacted with the doll's house and figures to build scenes that reflected their ideas of what museums – in a general sense, rather than reflecting on a particular institution – 'should be, represent and offer' (Mannay, 2019b, p 328). The three-storey doll's house acted as an analogy for the structure of museum spaces, and some young people demarcated the spaces by placing figures representing management on the top floor, metaphors of the public-facing museum on the middle floor, and symbols of the backstage spaces of the museum on the ground floor. The activity was presented without instructions about how or where the figures and objects should be located. However, the split structure of the doll's house facilitated young people to delineate different aspects of heritage sites in this way (Mannay, 2019c).

Young people compartmentalised organisational aspects of museums within each of the three floors. However, they also made connections between these separate floors by utilising fencing from the sandboxing objects to illustrate how the different floors could actively communicate with each other. Consequently, the doll's house afforded opportunities for young people to communicate the ways in which the public may be unaware of the work done by curators, researchers, and conservators behind the scenes (Mannay, 2019b).

In addition to the three-storey structure of the doll's house, each floor of the doll's house was also separated by walls into two different rooms. This structural feature facilitated young people to create a contrasting representation in each room. For example, in one of the interviews participants populated the two rooms on the top floor to visualise two contrasting views of management. One room featured identical wooden peg figures as a representation of a conventional management system. The adjoining room was populated with a diverse range of figures that symbolised hopes that organisational systems would evolve to ensure that individuals with different backgrounds, including young people, would have an active voice on management boards in the future.

The parallel rooms on each floor created an opportunity 'not just to represent one idea of what a museum could be, but to present alternative forms of the idea of a museum, which is more resonant with the diversity of the heritage and arts landscape' (Mannay, 2019b, p 328). The study also engaged with museum staff who interacted with the doll's house to share their

Figure 4.2: 'It springs from your box'

perspectives on the purpose of the heritage sector and the role of museums. With this participant group, the floors and rooms were also used to demarcate spaces, but each participant brought a unique perspective. For example, as illustrated in Figure 4.2, in one interview the tray that Dawn had transported the figures in was placed on the ground floor to symbolise how the museum 'springs from your box', emphasising the importance of collections and how the collections of individual museums to some extent define the story that can be told within particular heritage sites (Mannay, 2019c, p 129).

In this study, the structure of the doll's house, rather than the more open space of the sandbox, proved useful for participants to think through heritage and the roles and purposes of museum spaces. Therefore, it may be useful to explore different modes and mediums in which figures and objects can be presented in relation to the aims of specific projects. The housing of figures then is open to adaption, as are the figures and objects themselves, as will be explored in the following section.

Changing the figures

In Chapter 2, we identified that alongside the sand tray, water, and miniature figures and objects, Lowenfeld (1939) also provided a range of art-based materials, including coloured paper, coloured and plain sticks, plasticine, and glitter. The case studies documented in Chapter 3 did not all offer additional materials as standard practice; but in cases where plasticine and coloured paper were to hand, they have been utilised by participants.

For example, in Catt Turney's study (2021) exploring Welsh children's school transitions, participants were provided with sand trays and figures, alongside a bag of additional creative arts and crafts materials. As a resolution to their frustration with the gendered stereotypes in a standardised sandboxing kit, one of the participants used plasticine to modify one of the 'girl' figures by attaching a cutlass sword to its hand. As illustrated in Figure 4.3, in this example the plasticine was used as a form of glue to attach the cutlass sword from a male figurine to the participant's selected miniature figure.

This is resonant of an adaption to the homemade kit created by Dawn and Vicky for the *University Challenge* study outlined in Chapter 2. As illustrated in Figure 4.4, the Tinkerbell figure

Figure 4.3: Figure with cutlass sword (reproduced with permission from Catt Turney)

Figure 4.4: Tinkerbell

was sparsely dressed, which is common for Tinkerbell toys, but the figure was also slightly worse for wear with paint peeling away from her scant covering of clothing. The kit was taken by Dawn to a conference workshop event in Wales in which one of the delegates, somewhat upset by Tinkerbell's outfit, fashioned a dress from a coloured paper Post-it note and attached it to the Tinkerbell figure.

The choice of figures in many sandboxing sets can be viewed as problematic in relation to dominant conceptualisations of gender (Mannay and Turney, 2020). Additionally, even when sandboxing sets are purpose built by researchers, it can be difficult to source figures that do not represent versions of hyper-femininity and hegemonic masculinity (Owen Blakemore and Centers, 2005). Accordingly, these examples of adaptions would suggest that alongside the sandboxing kit, it would be useful to provide materials that can be used to change the figures, offering items that can alter their appearance, role, and purpose.

Following Lowenfeld's (1939) example, researchers can include coloured paper, plasticine, and other arts materials so that participants can augment figures and better align them with their own perspectives, symbolism, and metaphorical meaning making. An expansion in arts materials is something that researchers could consider so that participants have the creative agency to make adaptions and additions. However, while these augmentations have been useful in relation to gendered issues, they may not be as effective in tackling the problematic absences of other signifiers such as ethnicity and disability.

In Chapter 3, the work of Jess Mannion (2023; 2024) was introduced, and rather than simply relying on the opportunities for adaption with arts materials, she supplemented her sandboxing kit by purchasing additional figures representing a range of disabilities. Dawn had also purchased the same figures to represent disability, as well as sourcing figures to represent different ethnicities to extend and supplement the standard sandboxing kit. These figures increase the diversity of figures offered to participants. However, the specific packs of figures that symbolise diversity can be significantly larger than the standard figures provided with portable sand tray kits, as illustrated in Figure 4.5. The sizing of these figures has not been directly raised by the participants that Dawn has worked with, yet this could be seen as problematic with regard to size being an indicator of a difference between some figures and others.

Despite the opportunities to adapt figures to challenge gendered assumptions or alter their presentation, as noted in this section, researchers have also expanded the figures in their collection in response to gendered absences. For example, Rhiannon Maniatt (forthcoming) undertook pilot studies using sandboxing before the main stage of data generation with Domestic Abuse Advocates (DAAs) in Wales, exploring their experiences of vicarious trauma and vicarious resilience. In the pilot study, it was noted that although there was a Superman figure in the sandboxing kit, there was no corresponding woman superhero. In response to this feedback, a Batgirl figure was added. Pilot participants also suggested that it would be useful to have more pet figures and

Figure 4.5: Size differences in sets of figures

more figures to represent artistic creativity, resulting in a dog figure and a small pack of children's crayons being sourced and added to the available figure options. These additional figures were later incorporated in the sand scenes created by the participants in the main study (Maniatt, 2023).

This section has discussed how figures can be augmented using coloured paper and plasticine, and the potential to source additional figures to address questions of diversity, absence, and preference. Yet, it may be beneficial not to try and have a 'figure that will represent everything and everyone, as this could potentially close down the potential to creatively work with metaphors, which is a key strength of sandboxing' (Mannay and Turney, 2020, p 242). It may also be useful for researchers to explore how sandboxing could be undertaken with objects only, removing the inclusion of figures representing people. As discussed in Chapter 2, in the initial sandboxing equipment collated by Dawn and Vicky there were a large number of benign objects such as paperclips, buttons and beads, which participants incorporated in their sand scenes; but figures representing people were also popular. This suggests that there is not necessarily an optimal sandboxing kit that will suit all studies, researchers, and participants, rather this is something that needs to be considered on a case-by-case basis.

Impact figures

The focus of this chapter so far has been on sandboxing as a means of data generation, but sandboxing equipment can also be useful in projects of dissemination, engagement, and impact. This book can be considered as a form of methodological dissemination, and as outlined in Chapter 1, we sandboxed the book to consider scope, context, and what we wanted to include and achieve with this publication. Accordingly, sandboxing was used not to produce data but to help us to think through and develop this book, which usefully illustrates the potential of the method as a planning and design tool for writing projects.

Images of sandboxing also feature in this book to better engage and communicate salient points to readers. Of course, taking photographs of visual materials flattens out the materiality of the activity, modifying what was photographed from three to two dimensions (Rose, 2016, p 33). Images are often published in black and white, replacing colour with tone and creating a different ambience. Additionally, photographs are unable to convey embodied experiences of being in the moment with an array of sensory input beyond the visual. Nonetheless, they remain a useful vehicle for bringing readers closer to the worlds created by participants by illustrating the use of metaphors created with figures and objects, and demonstrating how sand is used to communicate particular narratives. For example, arguably the inclusion of Figure 4.1 earlier in the chapter, in combination with the text-based description, offered readers a more nuanced understanding of Sarah's experience of being in a 'no man's land'.

As Kara et al (2021, p 122) note, 'our reporting, if we are sufficiently skilled and persuasive, may influence others', and the figures from sandboxing projects have also featured in multimodal outputs to share the key messages from research projects. This sharing process can be seen as one way to address the criticism that research projects accrue the most benefit for the researcher (Hugman et al, 2011), as while researchers may achieve accolades, publications and promotions linked to their projects, the communities that they work with may not see any positive outcomes or changes. This aligns with the idea of the 'researcher as a vampire' (Ward, 2015, p 170), as at the end of the project, 'once they have filled their bags, they escape with the loot, never to be seen again' (Gobo, 2008, p 306).

There are key tensions between listening and hearing and the extent to which the experiences, perspectives, and recommendations generated by participants can and do influence policy and practice (Lundy, 2007; Alexandra, 2015; Mannay et al, 2019b; Chicken et al, 2024). Consequently, it is important to explore different ways to advocate for the rights and interests of participants (Hugman et al, 2011), and to attempt to engage in a process of benefit sharing, where 'participants ... should benefit from research equally with researchers' (Kara et al, 2021, p 141). Finding ways to inform policy and practice can involve moving 'beyond the academic article' (Mannay 2019b, p 659), and this is where sandboxing figures can be repurposed.

As noted in Chapter 2, Dawn was involved in a series of research studies and associated activities with care-experienced children and young people in Wales, some of which contributed to a Research Excellence Framework (REF) Impact Case Study (Mannay et al, 2015; Mobedji and Mannay, 2018; Roberts et al, 2020; Boffey et al, 2021; Mannay et al, 2022). In these projects the research teams had been disappointed that despite the many excellent studies we read as part of reviewing the literature, there had been little change in the entrenched and pervasive inequalities faced by children and young people who are care-experienced. Furthermore, participants had challenged us about what we were going to do with the accounts that they shared with us and what would change (Mannay, 2023).

For these reasons, following the Mannay et al (2015) project the research team was invested in finding ways to share messages from children and young people and connect with diverse audiences, to influence not just policy but everyday practice on the ground in the fields of education and social care. As we had worked with care-experienced participants, it was also particularly important that any projects of dissemination, impact and engagement were careful to retain their anonymity, which generated some key challenges. All of the outputs from the project could not contain images of the participants or use their voices, but we were committed to all of the materials retaining traces of the children and young people that could communicate their key messages about what needed to change.

In addition to the standard reports, book chapters and journal articles, a number of multi-modal materials were created to try and reach different audiences including magazines for foster carers, magazines for care-experienced young people, artworks, music videos, animations, short films, and a web platform[1] (see Mannay, 2019b; Mannay et al, 2019b). In text-based outputs, images of the sand tray scenes were included to illustrate what children and young people had created, alongside the relevant transcribed conversations from the elicitation interviews. Alongside other images, the objects and figures used with the sand trays also played a role in four of the short films that we produced from the Mannay et al (2015) project. These visual elements were accompanied by readings of the interview text taken from the project report (Mannay et al, 2015), voiced by children and young people not involved in the research study.

Children and young people in the study articulated aspirations for their future with enthusiasm and confidence, expressing career ambitions similar to those anticipated by children who are not care-experienced. Therefore, we wanted to develop a film that emphasised the agency and ambition of participants, before exploring the barriers that children and young people who are care-experienced can face in educational systems. In some parts of this film, the figures and objects that children and young people used in their sand scenes were drawn on directly in conjunction with the audio of the interview transcript acted out by children and young people who were not participants in the study.

For example, the script notes for the film on future aspirations, as with all four of the linked series of films from the project, included annotations for the filmmakers. These annotations ensured that the filmmakers were aware of which participants used which figures, indicated by the pseudonyms participants had selected and their age, and how they were relevant to their narratives.

> This is what I want to be when I'm older: a hero. I would join the police or something. I also want to be a builder of stuff, a machine builder. So, then I can change the

world. Because that's what heroes do, change the world. (Thor, age 14) (Superman figure used in sand scene)

When I'm older I want to be in the army. Because there's some little wars which are going on and people are trying to fight for their country to keep it and I want to stay there. I want to help them and keep them going so that's why I want to be in the army… because the army fight wars and keep the countries nice and like better places for us all. (Bishop, age 11) (army figures used in sand scene)

The film featuring the first interview excerpt included the same Superman figure that Thor had drawn on to create his sand scene. However, to be engaging and hold the attention of the viewer, the films needed to be active rather than static and they included a series of images. In the example from Thor, the first sentence is accompanied with the Superman figure centralised. For the second sentence, a figure of a policemen is featured. When building is mentioned, the film then cuts to a shot of the clay building activity that children and young people could take part in as one of the various creative options that we offered to children in all-day sessions, which also included bag making, bead work, and T-shirt printing.

The film accompanying the second interview extract initially included soldier figures that were situated within Bishop's sand scene. Rather than focussing on isolated individual figures, the entire sand scene featuring the soldiers was centralised in the film shot. The accompanying narrative was then supported with a single knight warrior to illustrate 'war', and single soldier to represent 'fight'. The phrase 'better places for us all' was spoken with the backdrop of a collection of trees, and 'I want to help them', was a shot of a range of figures of people, as illustrated in Figure 4.6.

In these two cases, the figures and objects that participants drew on in the sandboxing activity were featured in the film, albeit intermingled with other images to engage the viewer and make the experience of the film aesthetically effective. However, not all participants took part in creative activities, so there were no associated material items to support their interview extracts.

Adaptions and developments

Figure 4.6: 'I want to help them'

For example, the following excerpt used in a film from the same project, which focused on what participants felt needed to be changed, was drawn from a group interview transcript, where a 16-year-old young person was reflecting on barriers to education and the inequalities faced by those within the care system.

> If you're moved out of county then one county will argue with the other county about who pays for transport, who pays for the schooling, who pays for food, who pays for everything that has something to do with your education. Councils are just like: 'no that's your problem, no that's your problem', palming young people off sort of thing and it's just really unpleasant. You know it shouldn't have to be, 'oh you're paying for it, you're paying for it', you know? It's a child, it's a human being.

The young person's account effectively communicates how being embroiled in the accounting practices between different local authorities within the care system had adverse impacts. However, there were no associated visual artefacts that had been selected by the young person to illustrate this point. In this case, selected figures from the sandboxing set were used in the film as illustrative metaphors, and the sequence of 'who pays for' and 'no that's your problem' went back and forth between two fantasy styled figures, shot in the style of a conversation.

The creation of these films, and more widely any multimodal outputs to communicate research findings, is not without issue as such outputs are 'a re-representation and revisualization of participants' accounts' (Mannay, 2019b, p 664). The words themselves were taken directly from participants' accounts, but they are not fully in context without the entire interview transcript. Furthermore, children and young people outside of the project, rather than the participants, were trained to become actors and narrate the excerpts used in the films. Some 'voice actors' were care-experienced, while others were not, and voices were not always well matched, with the accent, tone, and emphasis varying from the original interviews (Mannay et al, 2019a). It was impossible to recreate the depth of meaning from the original accounts in this retelling, and in listening to the films, there is a disjuncture between what was said, the way it was said, and the final film.

The same can be said of the participants' sandboxing and their use of the objects and figures in their sand scenes. The film images of sandboxing apparatus were mainly drawn from photographs, and returning to Rose's (2016, p 33) critique, photographs modify what was photographed from three to two dimensions, and then they are modified a second time in the filmmaking process. Rather than a direct representation, the contents of the sand scenes were edited in relation to the mode of media of their presentation, as well as being joined by images that were not in the context of participants' sand scenes, and in some cases not associated with participants' interview accounts.

Yet, as Kara et al (2021, p 122) contend, 'reporting on research is a powerful act' but 'with this power ... comes responsibility'; and maintaining anonymity and confidentiality was essential in relation to the circumstances of the participants and the ethical agreements set out within the study. The images of sandboxing figures and objects and the accompanying audio of the film were projects of revisualisation and revocalisation, which could only 'retain traces of the participants and enable a differential, and partial, form of authentic voice' (Mannay, 2019b, p 685). Nonetheless, even with this partiality the film outputs were welcomed by participants, and they have reached viewers who may not have engaged with the related reports and journal articles and made impacts on practice in the fields of education and social care. Therefore, it is worth considering not only how sandboxing may help to generate data but also how it can be utilised in projects of engagement, dissemination, and impact.

Conclusion

This chapter introduced adaptions and developments to the sandboxing method. It began by reflecting on the affordances of adding water to sand to create a consistency that enables the demarcations of areas within the tray and the construction of stable buildings and landscapes. The addition of water was based on the foundational work of Margaret Lowenfeld, and its adoption in the *Difficult Conversations* project suggested that participants were able to incorporate design elements that were important to their sand scenes, but that would not have been possible with dry sand.

However, in writing this chapter and considering the use of water, we have spoken to arts psychotherapists and play therapists who have shared their experiences of clients flooding the sand tray. This issue resonates with our reservations related to the practicalities of undertaking sandboxing as a form of qualitative research outlined in Chapter 2. Therefore, although useful, whether or not water is introduced may depend on how many sand trays you have available and the scheduling of interviews, as design decisions are both philosophically informed and necessarily practical.

As well as adding to the sandboxing apparatus, as in the example of water, it can also be useful to take away standard forms of equipment and replace them with alternatives. This was illustrated with the introduction of a three-storey doll's house in the museum study, which enabled participants to interact with a structure that perhaps better resonated with the aims and research questions of that particular study. It is worth noting that in Figure 4.2, the participant still utilised the sand tray that was used to transport the figures to the interview. This is a reminder of the need for flexibility and enabling spaces where participants can respond to activities in their own way, creating idiosyncratic, individual representations of their experiences in relation to the topic, rather than being prescriptive with the equipment that is provided. The chapter also offered examples of the innovative methods participants have employed to overcome issues of representation using Post-it notes and plasticine.

Lastly, the chapter reflected on how sandboxing can be used to plan writing projects, such as in our sandboxing of the book documented in Chapter 1, how photographs of sand scenes can generate a more nuanced understanding for readers of outputs, and how sandboxing figures can play a role in projects of engagement and impact. The key message from the chapter is that each use of sand and figures should be considered in relation to the specificities of each project and its potential participants. Therefore, researchers and participants should be provided with the space required for imagination, innovation, and playfulness to flourish, rather than being tied to set conventions; and we will look forward to seeing further sandboxing adaptions and developments in the future.

5

Conclusion

Chapter summary

Having arrived at the concluding chapter, we hope that this book has already provided readers with insights into the development of and the doing of sandboxing, both from our own practice and the examples of the work of other researchers who undertake qualitative interviewing with sand, objects, and figures. This final concluding chapter will draw together key strands from the book. It will then consider how sandboxing may be taken forward in the future and invite you as the reader to contemplate the ways in which you could adopt, adapt, and advance sandboxing in your ongoing research journeys.

Reflections on the book

In summarising the voyage of the book, we return to the introductory chapter where we discussed what we wanted the book to offer its readers. Our aims were outlined in relation to our sandboxing of the book, and Figure 5.1 provides a reminder of these aims. We will revisit these aims throughout this chapter, but it is important first to reflect on the relational qualities of sandboxing.

In thinking through relational materialism, Taguchi (2011) discusses the image of a child playing with sand, arguing that in a taken-for-granted gaze the viewer may comprehend the representation of an active subject who handles the passive sand. In this interpretation, the sand and the sandbox create a passive

Figure 5.1: Reflecting on sandboxing this book

backdrop for the active human subject, but Taguchi (2011) argues for a recognition of the agency of the sand itself.

> ... the sand is understood to play with the girl just as much as the girl is seen as playing with the sand. We think that the playing is taking place in-between the girl and the sand. We contend that there is no clear border between them in this event. The force of the girl's body and the force of the sand overlap and extend onto and into each other. Each change in either of them will resonate in the other. (Taguchi, 2011, p 38)

For Taguchi (2011) the sand is positioned as active because it asks the child specific questions and formulates problems to be solved, such as how the sand can be contained or poured. Therefore, it is beneficial to consider agency as relational, between people and things, as well as people and people; and in sandboxing note what happens between sand tray, sand, objects, researchers, and participants, with the interplay of these agentic actors foregrounded. Additionally, it is important to reflect on where methodological techniques originate from and the extent to which the agency of past approaches acts to influence their contemporary applications. Therefore, it is necessary to have some understanding of historical applications to inform how sandboxing can be applied in the present.

In sandboxing the book, one reason for including the set of three trees featured in Figure 5.1 was that they were symbolic of sandboxing being rooted in Indigenous knowledges, therapeutic practice, and qualitative inquiry. Similarly, the handcuffs were placed in the sand tray to emphasise that the story of sandboxing should be presented with reference to the historical narratives and approaches that acted as a springboard to its use in qualitative research. As Dahal and Gautam (2024, p 25) contend, 'there is no critical thinking without context', and Chapter 2 was concerned with providing a contextual foundation for readers to draw on to understand how sandboxing was developed and to consider the extent to which their adoption of the technique would entail a distancing from or embracing with elements of this philosophical and practice based legacy.

Chapter 2 acknowledged the central role of sand and objects in Indigenous knowledge transmission and creation; however, for a more nuanced understanding of the philosophy of sand talk, and research and Indigenous peoples more widely, we would direct readers to the broader literature base (see Green, 2014; Yunkaporta, 2019; Smith, 2021; Tempone-Wiltshire, 2024). In this chapter there was also a detailed discussion of the psychoanalytically informed conceptual frames and therapeutic practice, which formed the basis of the sandboxing apparatus. There was recognition of the influence of the psychoanalysts Sigmund Freud, Melanie Klein, Anna Freud, as well as key names in sand tray therapy and Sandplay, including Virginia Axline and Dora Kalff. Nonetheless, the chapter was mainly concerned with Margaret Lowenfeld's World Technique, which formed the material basis for the sandboxing apparatus.

The blue alien in Figure 5.1 was featured in the sand tray to remind us as authors of how unfamiliar ideas, terms and concepts can be alienating. Accordingly, we set out to offer scaffolding to support the reader unfamiliar with psychoanalytically informed qualitative research methods, rather than using unexplained jargon and making assumptions about previous knowledge. In Chapter 2, with the introduction of conceptual frames, it was particularly helpful to hold the blue alien in mind and try to think about how our description could be read and understood. Therefore, we hope that readers have been able to gain adequate information with enough clarity to enable decisions to be made about how conceptual links to therapeutic practice play into contemporary approaches in sandboxing.

This chapter also introduced readers to our first project involving sand, figures, and objects as part of the qualitative interviewing process with mature undergraduate students. Again, the blue alien was in mind, and we were careful to document how our homemade sandboxing kit came together, listing the complete set of figures and objects in Tables 2.1 and 2.2 to be clear about our original apparatus. This attention to clarity was also linked to the grains of sand in the glass bottle in Figure 5.1. In sandboxing the book, the bottled sand related to our aim that any ambiguity around sandboxing was countered by the representation of grains of sand as grains of truth. We had wanted the book to move beyond the partial truths of what went wrong and could have been better, offering readers an honest, reflexive, and critical account of our own practice. We hope that this has been achieved with our openness around our anxieties about the figures and objects we have offered in projects, our decisions not to use water despite it being centralised in the World Technique, our failure to notice Tinkerbell's peeling paint wardrobe malfunction (see Figure 4.4), and other small points of reflection throughout the book.

The ethical tensions associated with taking apparatus that originated in psychoanalytically informed therapeutic spaces and utilising it as a qualitative tool of data generation were also discussed in Chapter 2. For us, this origination was not a barrier to adopting sandboxing, rather we have been more interested in situated ethics, considering the communities that we work with, offering choice, and being attentive to the potential unintended consequences of new topics being introduced when participants lead the sandboxing activity and its accompanying narrative.

As participants can direct the sand scene conversation, this suggests that there are participatory elements of the sandboxing technique. The glass bottle filled with sand and corked to maintain separation in Figure 5.1 is also suggestive of sandboxing's participatory potential. The separation of the sand in the bottle can be seen as illustrative of what is placed in the tray and what is shared, and also how the metaphoric quality of the apparatus means that participants can change their mind about the narrative of an object. Therefore, participants have an element of control over holding back, altering, or communicating the original meaning that they assigned to their figures and objects. Accordingly, the book has explored the relationship with sandboxing and participatory approaches, contending that the technique can be drawn on in participatory projects, but that sandboxing in itself cannot be seen as necessarily participatory; and that we need to consider participatory practice as on a continuum rather than an either/or basis.

Returning to Figure 5.1, the trees and the eggs were also selected because they were the same category of object yet different in pigmentation. This was an analogy for the flexibility of sandboxing and its adaptability to different participants, contexts, and research questions. The usefulness of sandboxing across different academic disciplines, fields of interest, and communities was evidenced in the examples presented in Chapter 3. The chapter introduced studies with Queer Latinx men in Australia (Haro, 2022), people with intellectual disabilities in Ireland (Mannion, 2024), young parents in Wales (Mannay et al, 2018a), as well as other distinct geographical and topic-based research. The basket featured in Figure 5.1 was about others not just taking the sandboxing method as part of their toolbox of creative methods, but also combining sandboxing with other techniques. This combined approach was also seen in Chapter 3, with, for example, Catt Turney's heavy bag of creative activities that they managed to keep intact as they negotiated complicated journeys on public transport and long walks to participants' homes (Turney, 2021).

The basket and eggs nearby in the Figure 5.1 sand scene also resonate with the colloquial phrase 'don't put all your eggs in one basket'. This has been a guiding principle in the book as it was important to again emphasise the need to be open to opportunities to diversify sandboxing to suit the needs of individual projects. As showcased in Chapter 4, researchers have worked with sandboxing in novel and innovative ways such as introducing water to the sand tray (Watson et al, 2021; Staples et al, 2024) and using sandboxing figures as tools of dissemination, engagement, and impact (Mannay et al, 2019b). Those participating in sandboxing have also been creative, as demonstrated with the design and fitting of a Post-it note dress for the Tinkerbell miniature character (Figure 4.4) and the securing of a cutlass sword to a figure using plasticine (Figure 4.3). In this way, Chapter 4 was very much concerned with the opportunity to share ongoing developments with sandboxing and to inspire others to continue to innovate and to improve sandboxing techniques.

The chess pieces in Figure 5.1 were included as a reminder to be careful and considered in writing this book, to do justice to the sandboxing technique and illustrate its value as a tool to support qualitative interviewing. We also wanted to align this book with the aims of Helen Kara's Creative Research Methods in Practice Policy Press series, which are outlined in this blog excerpt.

> I wanted to edit this series because there are no such books available to help researchers learn in detail about why, when, and how to use a new research method. There are several books giving an overview of creative research methods, within or across academic disciplines: some sole-authored, some edited collections. These are useful texts, but they do not generally offer enough depth of information to enable readers to try out the methods for themselves with confidence. The main rationale for this new series is to do just that. (Kara, 2023, n.p.)

This is, to our knowledge, the first book dedicated to sandboxing as a qualitative research method, and aligning with the aim of the series, we have hopefully provided sufficient information about sandboxing for others to try this with some confidence in the future. The future of sandboxing will be discussed further in the following and final section of the book.

Where next with sandboxing?

Hopefully, the preceding chapters have communicated our own enthusiasm for sandboxing, visualised in Vicky's heart and Dawn's champagne bottle in our sandboxing of the book (Figure 5.1), as well as sparking interest in you as readers. While writing this book, we have engaged with others who are curious about adopting sandboxing in workshops, online meetings and in-person chats. Our sandboxing kits have been borrowed by colleagues, doctoral students, and teams involved in engagement activities and public involvement.

Sometimes our sandboxing kits have been returned with some objects and figures missing. This is to be expected as desired objects can end up in the pockets of participants, a temptation we emphasise with ourselves; and in our own work, the odd shiny stone or fairy princess has disappeared. Items can also be left under a table or down the edge of a sofa, depleting the available resources for sandboxing. However, we have also been gifted with additions to our equipment as with the adaptions made by Rhiannon Maniatt (2023) discussed in Chapter 4, which added some useful options for future 'sandboxers'.

You may then be thinking about creating your own sandboxing kit. This could be constructed from miscellaneous objects as in Tables 2.1 and 2.2 in Chapter 2, or purchased from a sand tray supplier, and perhaps supplemented with additional figures to increase the diversity of options for participants to identify with and act as representations of their lives and experiences. If this is the case, and you have your materials ready, then there are some further points you may want to consider before you take your version of sandboxing apparatus out into the world.

In the 'Methods for Change' project, Laura Pottinger and colleagues (2022), interviewed academics about their use of creative and qualitative methodologies. In this process they asked the participants to select an object that they could use to talk about their research method. The activity enabled these researcher participants to be reflexive and consider aspects of their work that could have remained unspoken, and many enjoyed the activity, but there were also instances of awkwardness in these creative moments. These responses were an important consideration for the research team, who reflected that 'trepidation about talking through objects raises questions about what academics tend to expect of participants, or assume they will find "meaningful," yet may be less prepared to do themselves' (Pottinger et al, 2022, p 16).

This is a valuable point, which highlights the usefulness of becoming a 'participant' and trying out sandboxing yourself, and preferably doing this with other people. In teaching and in workshops we ask people to engage with activities, whether this be to draw a picture, make zines, create a fuzzy felt scene, or engage in sandboxing. We then ask people to share what they have made and discuss it with others in the group. The rationale for trying things out and sharing what they have made is that we should not ask participants to do things that we are not prepared to do ourselves, and in the doing of activities we gain insights into what may be a potential site of trepidation.

Adriana Haro (2022) attended workshops and tried out different creative methods to inform the type of techniques that they would feel comfortable with using prior to commencing their research with Queer Latinx men in Australia. In a drawing activity, they felt uneasy about others seeing what they had drawn, and in using LEGO® with a group, thought that the process required a significant level of imagination, meaning that they began feeling 'lost' (Harro, 2022, p 99). This process of exploration enabled them to develop an affinity with sandboxing, providing a secure base from which to facilitate this technique with participants.

The piloting of the activity with communities who share similarities with the participants you intend to work with also brings opportunities for new perspectives to feed into planning and contingency measures. There will still be new issues that arise, but these preparatory activities offer a foundation for dealing with the unexpected or unintended elements of research and increase confidence in facilitating sandboxing.

This confidence is also important in making a method your own. This book has shared ideas and advice to reflect on, but it should not be read as a prescribed fixed list that should be rigidly followed. As Pickering (2008, p 5) contends, 'methods are guidelines for practice, and researchers should feel free to adopt them to suit their purposes'; as well as adopting, we would add adapting. Consequently, we would encourage readers to build on and refine sandboxing so that it best fits with the topic explored and the communities engaged in projects. Researchers have expertise in their own fields that can be drawn on to foster different ways of working and, as illustrated in the work of Jess Mannion (2024) outlined in Chapter 3, co-inquires can also contribute to the design, data production, analysis, and dissemination of projects that make use of sandboxing.

Returning to Pickering (2008, p 4), we can combine methods rather than being confined to one technique of data generation, and this pluralist approach means that 'the strengths of one method may help overcome the limitations of another', making it easier to build a more nuanced understanding of the topic under exploration. This book has showcased studies that have introduced sandboxing along with techniques including timelines, collage, drawing, poetry, and LEGO®. These examples demonstrate the ways in which sandboxing can be effectively combined with other creative and qualitative methods, as well as showcasing how sandboxing equipment itself can be used in different ways with the addition of water, plasticine, and Post-it notes.

We have been continually impressed with the developments in sandboxing that we have witnessed since our initial endeavours with a repurposed wooden drawer, a bag of play sand, and objects foraged from our homes. It has been particularly pleasing to see people who have attended our workshop or read our papers go on to inject innovation, imagination, and ingenuity into their practices of data generation, analysis, and impact. As we documented in Chapter 1, the trees featured in Figure 5.1 were visualised as continually developing and branching in new directions and the accompanying eggs poised to reveal new forms of life. Consequently, as we hand over to you as the readers of this book, we are excited to see 'where next with sandboxing' and we look forward to reading future publications where researchers report on their *Qualitative Interviewing with Sand, Objects, and Figures.*

Notes

Chapter 2

1. The Rorschach ink blot test was first developed by Hermann Rorschach in 1921 and it has been used extensively by psychiatrists, clinical psychologists, and psychometricians and in the United Kingdom it was popular within institutions such as the Tavistock and Child Guidance Clinics. The Rorschach ink blot test consists of '10 ink blots 'plates' upon which the person 'projects' what they can 'see'. In the same way that one can look up at the sky and 'see' a dinosaur in the clouds, one can look at the ambiguous ink blot stimuli and say what they 'see" (Hubbard, 2016, p 7).
2. The five stages of psychosexual development set out by Freud were the oral stage, anal stage, phallic stage, latency, and the genital stage. For more information about Freud's developmental theory and approach to psychoanalysis, see Milton et al (2011) for an introductory text to this work.
3. There is no space in this volume to provide a full account of development of Sandplay as a tool of Jungian therapy and its contemporary international use as a therapeutic tool. Therefore, we would recommend the comprehensive scholarship of Barbara A. Turner (2023) for readers interested in finding out more about Jungian Sandplay.
4. A metaphor is something used, or regarded as being used, to represent something else as a symbolic representation. For example, in sandboxing the literal meaning of a figure or object placed in the sand tray does not necessarily align with the meaning attached to the figure or object by the participant.

Chapter 4

1. Outputs from this project, including the film examples discussed in this chapter are available at https://www.exchangewales.org/lace/.

References

Adriansen, H. (2012) 'Timeline interviews: a tool for conducting life history research', *Qualitative Studies*, 3(1): 40–55.

Alexandra, D. (2015) 'Are we listening yet? Participatory knowledge production through media practice: Encounters of political listening', in A. Gubrium, K. Harper and M. Otanez (eds) *Participatory Visual and Digital Research in Action*, Walnut Creek, CA: Left Coast Press, pp 41–56.

Axline, V.M. (1947) *Play Therapy*, New York: Ballantine Books.

Axline, V.M. (1964) *Dibs: In Search of Self; Personality Development in Play Therapy*, London: Penguin Books.

Bacic, R. (2013) 'Arpilleras: evolution and revolution' Keynote Paper and Exhibition, *3rd International Visual Methods Conference*, Victoria University of Wellington, Wellington, New Zealand, 2–6 September 2013, https://cain.ulster.ac.uk/quilts/exhibit/followup.html#wellington03091

Berends, L. (2011) 'Embracing the visual: using timelines with in-depth interviews on substance misuse and treatment', *The Qualitative Report*, 19(1): 1–9.

Bloor, M., Fincham, B. and Sampson, H. (2010) 'Unprepared for the worst: risks of harm for qualitative researchers', *Methodological Innovations Online*, 5(1): 45–55.

Boffey, M., Mannay, D., Vaughan, R. and Wooders, C. (2021) *The Fostering Communities Programme – Walking Tall: Stage One Evaluation*. Project Report, Cardiff: The Fostering Network in Wales.

Braun, V. and Clarke, V. (2006) 'Using thematic analysis in psychology', *Qualitative Research Psychology*, 3(2): 77–101.

Braun, V. and Clarke, V. (2021) 'One size fits all? What counts as quality practice in (reflexive) thematic analysis?', *Qualitative Research in Psychology*, 18(3): 328–352.

Broomfield, K. (2024) 'Analysing the unspoken: finding the richness created in dialogue with people who cannot speak', in H. Kara, D. Mannay and A.N. Roy (eds) *Handbook of Creative Data Analysis*, Bristol: Policy Press, pp 405–421.

Burnard, P. (2018) 'Arts-based research methods: a brief overview', Creative Research Methods Symposium, 2 July 2018, University of Derby.

Busher, H. and James, N. (2018) 'Struggling for selfhood: non-traditional mature students: critical perspectives on access to Higher Education courses', in R. Waller, N. Ingram and M. Ward (eds) *Higher Education and Social Inequalities: University Admissions, Experiences and Outcomes*, Abingdon: Routledge, https://doi.org/10.4324/9781315449722.

Carroll, K. (2018), 'Approaching bereavement research with heartfelt positivity', in T. Loughran and D. Mannay (eds) *Emotion and the Researcher: Sites, Subjectivities, and Relationships*, Studies in Qualitative Methodology, Bingley: Emerald, pp 97–111.

Carruthers Thomas, K. (2024) 'Five "Survive" Lockdown: revisualising survey data as a graphic novella', in H. Kara, D. Mannay and A. N. Roy (eds) *Handbook of Creative Data Analysis*, Bristol: Policy Press, pp 21–35.

Cattanach, A. (1992) *Play Therapy with Abused Children*, London: Jessica Kingsley.

Chadwick, R. (2021) 'Theorizing voice: toward working otherwise with voices', *Qualitative Research* 21(1): 76–101.

Chicken, S., Tur Porres, G., Mannay, D., Parnell, J. and Tyrie, J. (2024) 'Questioning "voice" and silence: Exploring creative and participatory approaches to researching with children through a Reggio Emilian lens', *Qualitative Research*, https://doi.org/10.1177/14687941241234299

Clark, A. (2020) 'Visual ethics beyond the crossroads', in L. Pauwels and D. Mannay (eds) *The Sage Handbook of Visual Research Methods* (2nd edn), London: Sage, pp 682–693.

Clark, A. and Moss, P. (2001) *Listening to Children: The Mosaic Approach*, London: National Children's Bureau.

Clarke, S. and Hoggett, P. (eds) (2009) *Researching Beneath the Surface: Psychosocial Research and Society: Methods in Practice*, London: Karnac.

References

Coffey, J., Senior, K., Haro, A., Farrugia, D., Threadgold, S., Cook, J. et al (2023) 'Embodying debt: youth, consumer credit and its impacts for wellbeing', *Journal of Youth Studies*, 27(5): 685–705.

Cram, F., Chilisa, B. and Mertens, D. (2013) 'The journey begins', in D. Mertens, F. Cram and B. Chilisa (eds) *Indigenous Pathways into Social Research: Voices of a New Generation*, Walnut Creek, CA: Left Coast Press, pp 11–40.

Dahal, B. and Gautam, S. (2024) 'Creative research methods in the geo-political South', in H. Kara (ed.), *The Bloomsbury Handbook of Creative Research Methods*, London: Bloomsbury, pp 21–30.

Davis, M. (1992) *Play and Symbolism in Lowenfeld and Winnicott*, Dr Margaret Lowenfeld Trust, https://lowenfeld.org/wp-content/uploads/2017/10/Play-and-symbolism-in-Lowenfeld-and-Winnicott-MadeleineDavis 1.pdf

Delamont, S. and Atkinson, P. (1995) *Fighting Familiarity: Essays on Education and Ethnography*, Cresskill, NJ: Hampton.

Dodding, J. and Partington, H. (2024) 'I poems and polyvocality: experiences of using a combined qualitative creative analysis technique to strengthen the voices of research participants and aid reflexivity', in H. Kara, D. Mannay and A. N. Roy (eds) *The Handbook of Creative Data Analysis*, Bristol: Policy Press, pp 223–234.

Dumangane, C. (2016) Exploring the Narratives of the few: British African Caribbean Male Graduates of Elite Universities in England and Wales, PhD Thesis, Cardiff University.

Dumangane, C. (2022) 'Cufflinks, photos and YouTube: the benefits of third object prompts when researching race and discrimination in elite higher education', *Qualitative Research*, 22(1): 3–23.

Eldén, S. (2012) 'Inviting the messy: drawing methods and "children's voices"', *Childhood*, 20(1): 66–81.

Ellis, K., Hickle, K. and Warrington, C. (2023) 'Researching sensitive topics with children and young people: ethical practice and blurry boundaries', *International Journal of Qualitative Methods*, 22: https://doi.org/10.1177/16094069231207011.

Folkes, L. (2015) 'Review Article Smith, J.A. (ed.) Qualitative Psychology: A Practical Guide to Research Methods', *Sociological Research Online*, https://www.socresonline.org.uk/21/2/reviews/5.html

Frosh, S. (2010) *Psychoanalysis Outside the Clinic: Interventions in Psychosocial Studies*, Basingstoke: Macmillan.

Frosh, S. and Emerson, P. (2005) 'Interpretation and over-interpretation: disrupting the meaning of texts', *Qualitative Research*, 5(5): 307–324.

Gabb, J. and Fink, J. (2015) 'Telling moments and everyday experience: multiple methods research on couple relationships and personal lives', *Sociology* 49(5): 970–987.

Gadd, D. and Jefferson, T. (2007) *Psychosocial Criminology*, London: Sage.

Gascoine, L., Wall, K. and Higgins, S. (2024) 'What can creative data analysis using word clouds tell us about student views of learning something new?', in H. Kara, D. Mannay and A.N. Roy (eds) *The Handbook of Creative Data Analysis*, Bristol: Policy Press, pp 65–82.

Gauntlett, D. and Holzwarth, P. (2006) 'Creative and visual methods for exploring identities', *Visual Studies*, 21(1): 82–91.

Gobo, G. (2008) 'Leaving the field', in G. Gobo (ed.) *Doing Ethnography*, London: Sage, pp 306–313.

Grant, A. (2018) 'Shock and offence online: the role of emotion in participant absent research', in T. Loughran and D. Mannay (eds) *Emotion and the Researcher: Sites, Subjectivities, and Relationships*, Studies in Qualitative Methodology, Bingley: Emerald, pp 143–158.

Grant, A., Mannay, D. and Marzella, R. (2018) '"People try and police your behaviour": the impact of surveillance on mothers' and grandmothers' perceptions and experiences of infant feeding', *Families, Relationships and Societies*, 7(3): 431–447.

Grant, A., Morgan, M., Mannay, D. and Gallagher, D. (2019) 'Understanding health behaviour in pregnancy and infant feeding intentions in low-income women from the UK through qualitative visual methods and application to the COM-B (Capability, Opportunity, Motivation – Behaviour) model', *BMC Pregnancy and Childbirth*, 19: 56, https://doi.org/10.1186/s12884-018-2156-8.

Grant, A., Morgan, M., Gallagher, D. and Mannay, D. (2020) 'Smoking during pregnancy, stigma and secrets: visual methods exploration in the UK', *Women and Birth*, 33(1): 70–76.

References

Gray, K. and Lazenby, E. (2024) 'The analogue journey method', in H. Kara, D. Mannay and A.N. Roy (eds) *The Handbook of Creative Data Analysis*, Bristol: Policy Press, pp 280–294.

Green, J. (2014) *Drawn from the Ground: Sound, Sign and Inscription in Central Australian Sand Stories*, Cambridge: Cambridge University Press.

Guillemin, M. and Drew, S. (2010) 'Questions of process in participant-generated visual methodologies', *Visual Studies*, 25(2): 175–188.

Haro, A. (2022) *Disidentifying Masculinities: Queer Latinx Embodiment in Australia*, PhD Thesis, University of Newcastle Australia.

Harper, D. (2023) *Visual Sociology* (2nd edn), London: Sage.

Harris, M. and Butterworth, G. (2002) *Developmental Psychology: A Student's Handbook*, Hove: Psychology Press.

Hart, R. (1992) *Children's participation: from tokenism to citizenship*, UNICEF Innocenti Essays, No. 4, Florence, Italy: International Child Development Centre of UNICEF.

Hodges, A.S. (2016) *The Family Centred Experiences of Siblings in the Context of Cystic Fibrosis: A Dramaturgical Exploration*, PhD Thesis, Cardiff University.

Hodges, A.S. (2018) 'The positional self and researcher emotion: Destabilising sibling equilibrium in the context of cystic fibrosis', in T. Loughran and D. Mannay (eds) *Emotion and the Researcher: Sites, Subjectivities, and Relationships, Vol. 16. Studies in Qualitative Methodology*, Bingley: Emerald, pp 49–63.

Hollway, W. (2011) 'Through discursive psychology to a psychosocial approach', in N. Bozatzis and T. Dragonas (eds), *Social Psychology: The Turn to Discourse*, Athens: Metaixmio, pp 209–240.

Hollway, W. and Jefferson, T. (2000) *Doing Qualitative Research Differently*, London: Sage.

Hollway, W. and Jefferson, T. (2001) 'Free association, narrative analysis and the defended subject: the case of Ivy', *Narrative Inquiry*, 11(1): 103–122.

Hollway, W. and Jefferson, T. (2005a) 'Panic and perjury: A psychosocial exploration of agency', *British Journal of Social Psychology*, 44(2): 147–163.

Hollway, W. and Jefferson, W. (2005b) 'But why did Vince get sick? A reply to Spears and Wetherell', *British Journal of Social Psychology*, 44(2): 175–180.

Hollway, W. and Jefferson, T. (2009) 'Researching defended subjects with the free association narrative interviewing method', in H.J. Cook, S. Bhattacharya and A. Hardy (eds), *History of the Social Determinants of Health: Global Histories, Contemporary Debates*, Hyderabad: Orient Black Swan, pp 296–315.

Hubbard, K. (2016) *A History of the Rorschach Ink Blot Test in Britain*, PhD Thesis, University of Surrey.

Hugman, R., Pittaway, E. and Bartolomei, L. (2011) 'When "do no harm" is not enough: the ethics of research with refugees and other vulnerable groups', *British Journal of Social Work*, 41(7): 1271–1287.

Hurdley, R. (2006) 'Dismantling mantelpieces: narrating identities and materializing culture in the home', *Sociology*, 40(4): 717–733.

Hutton, D. (2004) 'Margaret Lowenfeld's 'World Technique'', *Clinical Child Psychology and Psychiatry*, 9(4): 605–612.

Jayne, K., Pell, L., Power, N. and Stanhope, A. (2024) 'ARTiculating an ethical position: a group of arts psychotherapists use a collaborative arts-based (research) process to set their ethical scene when employing creative methods within mental health research' in H. Kara (ed.), *The Bloomsbury Handbook of Creative Research Methods*, London: Bloomsbury, pp 279–296.

John, Z. (2024) 'Grappling with poetry: why to start and how to start' in H. Kara (ed.), *The Bloomsbury Handbook of Creative Research Methods*, London: Bloomsbury, pp 95–106.

Kara, H. (2023) *Creative Research Methods in Practice*, online blog, 3 June 2023, https://helenkara.com/2023/06/01/creative-research-methods-in-practice/

Kara, H. (ed.) (2024a) *The Bloomsbury Handbook of Creative Research Methods*, London: Bloomsbury.

Kara, H. (2024b) *Personal communication to Dawn Mannay reflecting on a creative methods teaching workshop at University of Liverpool*, 28 May 2024.

Kara, H., Lemon, N., Mannay, D. and McPherson, M. (2021) *Creative Research Methods in Education: Principles and Practices*, Bristol: Policy Press.

Kara, H., Mannay, D. and Roy, A.N. (2024) *The Handbook of Creative Data Analysis*, Bristol: Policy Press.

Khoo, S. (2024) 'Creative research methods and ethics', in H. Kara (ed.) *The Bloomsbury Handbook of Creative Research Methods*, London: Bloomsbury, pp 9–20.

References

Klein, M. (1975) *Love, Guilt and Reparation, and Other Works, 1921–1945*, London: Hogarth Press.

Leigh, J.S., Hiscock, J.R., Koops, S., McConnell, A.J., Haynes, C.J.E., Caltagirone, C. et al (2024) 'Analysing creative multimodal data for a scientific audience', in H. Kara, D. Mannay and A.N. Roy (eds) *The Handbook of Creative Data Analysis*, Bristol: Policy Press, pp 83–100.

Lisiak, A. and Krzyżowski, L. (2018) 'With a little help from my colleagues: notes on emotional support in a qualitative longitudinal research project', in T. Loughran and D. Mannay (eds) *Emotion and the Researcher: Sites, Subjectivities, and Relationships*, Studies in Qualitative Methodology, Bingley: Emerald, pp 33–47.

Loewenthal, D. (2023) *The Handbook of Phototherapy and Therapeutic Photography*, Abingdon: Routledge.

Lomax, H. (2012) 'Contested voices? Methodological tensions in creative visual research with children', *International Journal of Social Research Methodology* 15(2): 105–117.

Loughran, T. and Mannay, D. (eds) (2018) *Emotion and the Researcher: Sites, Subjectivities, and Relationships*, Studies in Qualitative Methodology, Bingley: Emerald.

Lowenfeld, M. (1939) 'The world pictures of children', *British Journal of Medical Psychology*, 18(1): 65–101.

Lowenfeld, M. (1950) 'The nature and use of the Lowenfeld World Technique in work with children and adults', *The Journal of Psychology*, 30(2): 325–331.

Lowenfeld, M. (1979). *The World Technique*, London: Allen and Unwin Press.

Lundy, L. (2007) 'Voice is not enough: Conceptualising article 12 of the United Nations Convention on the Rights of the Child', *British Educational Research Journal*, 33(6): 927–942.

Lytje, M. and Holliday, C. (2022) 'Sand tray interviews: Developing a method to explore the grief and support needs of 4- to 8-year old parentally bereaved children', *Bereavement: Journal of Grief and Responses to Death*, 1: https://doi.org/10.54210/bj.2022.21.

Maniatt, R. (2023) 'Reflections on using the sandboxing technique in exploring vicarious trauma/resilience with domestic abuse advocates' presented at 23rd *Annual Conference of the European Society of Criminology*, Florence, Italy, 6–9 September 2023.

Maniatt, R. (forthcoming) 'It's Like Wading through Mud. But Pink, Glittery, Gorgeous Smelling Mud': An Exploration of Domestic Abuse Advocates' Experiences of Vicarious Trauma and Vicarious Resilience, PhD Thesis, Cardiff: Cardiff University.

Mannay, D. (2010) 'Making the familiar strange: can visual research methods render the familiar setting more perceptible?', *Qualitative Research*, 10(1): 91–111.

Mannay, D. (2013) 'Review of *Qualitative research methods in psychology* and *Qualitative methods in psychology: A research guide*, 2nd ed.', *Qualitative Research*, 13 (2): 242–244.

Mannay, D. (2016) *Visual, Narrative and Creative Research Methods: Application, Reflection and Ethics*, Abingdon: Routledge.

Mannay, D. (2018) "You just get on with it': negotiating the telling and silencing of trauma and its emotional impacts in interviews with marginalised mothers', in T. Loughran and D. Mannay (eds) *Emotion and the Researcher: Sites, Subjectivities, and Relationships*, Studies in Qualitative Methodology, Bingley: Emerald, pp 81–94.

Mannay, D. (2019a) 'Artefacts, third objects, sandboxing and figurines in the doll's house', in L. Pauwels and D. Mannay (eds) *The SAGE Handbook of Visual Research Methods* (2nd edn), London: SAGE Publications, pp 322–332.

Mannay, D. (2019b) 'Revisualizing data: engagement, impact and multimodal dissemination', in L. Pauwels and D. Mannay (eds) *The SAGE Handbook of Visual Research Methods* (2nd edn), London: SAGE Publications, pp 659–669.

Mannay, D. (2019c) *Hands on Heritage: Exploring Creative and Collaborative Approaches with Young People at the National Museum Wales*, Project Report, Cardiff: Amgueddfa Cymru – National Museum Wales.

Mannay, D. (2023) 'Déjà vu et jamais vu: What happens when the field expands in ways that mean there is no exit?', in R. Smith and S. Delamont (eds), *Leaving the Field: Methodological Insights from Ethnographic Exits*, Manchester: Manchester University Press, pp 113–125.

Mannay, D. and Edwards, V. (2015) 'Visual methods and the World Technique: the importance of the elicitation interview in understanding non-traditional students' journeys through university', *SAGE Research Methods Datasets*, http://dx.doi.org/10.4135/9781473938076

References

Mannay, D. and Creaghan, J. (2016) 'Similarity and familiarity: reflections on indigenous ethnography with mothers, daughters and school teachers on the margins of contemporary Wales, in M. Ward (ed.) *Gender Identity and Research Relationships*, Vol. 14. Studies in Qualitative Methods, Bingley: Emerald, pp 85–103.

Mannay, D. and Staples, E. (2019) 'Sandboxes, stickers and superheroes: Employing creative techniques to explore the aspirations and experiences of children and young people who are looked after', in D. Mannay, A. Rees and L. Roberts (eds) *Children and Young People 'Looked After'? Education, Intervention and the Everyday Culture of Care in Wales*, Cardiff: University of Wales Press, pp 169–182.

Mannay, D. and Hodges, A. (2020) '"Third objects" and sandboxes creatively engaging children to share their understandings of social worlds', in E.J. White (ed.), *Seeing the World through Children's Eyes: Visual Methodologies and Approaches to Early Learning*, Leiden: Brill, pp 25–40.

Mannay, D. and Turney, C. (2020) 'Sandboxing: a creative approach to qualitative research in education', in M. Ward and S. Delamont (eds) *Handbook of Qualitative Research in Education* (2nd edn), Cheltenham: Edward Elgar, pp 233–45.

Mannay, D. and Ward, M.R.M. (2020) 'The Coffee Club: An initiative to support mature and non-traditional higher education students in Wales', in G. Crimmins (ed.) *Strategies for Supporting Inclusion and Diversity in the Academy: Higher Education, Aspiration and Inequality*, London: Palgrave Macmillan, pp 225–248.

Mannay, D., Staples, E., Hallett, S., Roberts, L., Rees, A., Evans, R.E. et al (2015) *Understanding the Educational Experiences and Opinions, Attainment, Achievement and Aspirations of Looked After Children in Wales*, Project Report, Cardiff: Welsh Government.

Mannay, D., Staples, E. and Edwards, V. (2017) 'Visual methodologies, sand and psychoanalysis: employing creative participatory techniques to explore the educational experiences of mature students and children in care', *Visual Studies*, 32(4): 345–358.

Mannay, D., Creaghan, J., Gallagher, D., Marzella, R., Mason, S., Morgan, M. et al (2018a) 'Negotiating closed doors and constraining deadlines: the potential of visual ethnography to effectually explore private and public spaces of motherhood and parenting', *Journal of Contemporary Ethnography*, 47(6): 758–781.

Mannay, D., Creaghan, J., Gallagher, D., Mason, S., Morgan, M. and Grant, A. (2018b). "Watching what I'm doing, watching how I'm doing it': exploring the everyday experiences of surveillance and silenced voices among marginalised mothers in Welsh low-income locales', in T. Taylor and K. Bloch (eds) *Marginalized Mothers, Mothering from the Margins. Advances in Gender Research* Vol. 25. Bingley: Emerald, pp 25–40.

Mannay, D., Roberts, L., Staples, E. and Ministry of Life (2019a) 'Lights, camera, action: Translating research findings into policy and practice impacts with music, film and artwork', in D. Mannay, A. Rees and L. Roberts (eds), *Children and Young People 'Looked After'? Education, Intervention and the Everyday Culture of Care in Wales*, Cardiff: University of Wales Press, pp 210–224.

Mannay, D., Staples, E., Hallett, S., Roberts, L., Rees, A., Evans, R. et al (2019b) 'Enabling talk and reframing messages: working creatively with care experienced children and young people to recount and re-represent their everyday experiences', *Child Care in Practice*, 25(1): 51–63.

Mannay, D., Boffey, M., Cummings, A., Cunningham, E., Davies, B., Stabler, L. et al (2022) *The Strengths and Challenges of Online Services and Interventions to Support the Mental Health and Wellbeing of Care-experienced Children and Young People: A Study Exploring the Views of Young People, Carers, and Social Care Professionals in Wales during the Coronavirus Pandemic*, Project Report, Cardiff: The Fostering Network in Wales.

Mannion, J. (2023) *Establishing a Co-operative Inquiry Group for People with Intellectual Disabilities to Explore Relationships and Sexuality in their Lives*, PhD Thesis, Trinity College, the University of Dublin.

Mannion, J. and the R&S (Relationships and Sexuality) Research Team (2024) 'Creative collaborative data analysis: Co-constructing and co-analysing the data together', in H. Kara, D. Mannay and A. N. Roy (eds) *Handbook of Creative Data Analysis*, Bristol: Policy Press, pp 372–388.

McCann, I.L. and Pearlman, L.A. (1990) 'Vicarious traumatisation: a framework for understanding the psychological effects of working with victims', *Journal of Traumatic Stress*, 3(1): 131–149.

McEwan, C. (2003) 'Building a postcolonial archive? Gender, collective memory and citizenship in post-Apartheid South Africa', *Journal of Southern African Studies*, 29(3): 748.

Midgley, N. (2006) 'Psychoanalysis and qualitative psychology: complementary or contradictory paradigms?', *Qualitative Research in Psychology*, 3(3): 213–231.

Milton, J., Polmear, C. and Fabricius, J. (2011) *A Short Introduction to Psychanalysis* (2nd edn), Los Angeles: Sage.

Mobedji, S. and Mannay, D. (2018) *'Just listen': Care-experienced young people's views of the child protection system in Wales*, Project Report, Cardiff: The Fostering Network.

Morgan, M. (2016) 'Re-educating Rhian: Experiences of working-class mature student mothers', in D. Mannay (ed.) *Our Changing Land: Revisiting Gender, Class and Identity in Contemporary Wales*, Cardiff: University of Wales Press, pp 112–129.

Morgan, A., Davies, A.J. and Milton, E. (2024) 'Using discourse analysis to inform content analysis: a pragmatic, mixed-methods approach to exploring how the headteacher role is articulated in job descriptions', in H. Kara, D. Mannay and A. N. Roy (eds) *The Handbook of Creative Data Analysis*, Bristol: Policy Press, pp 50–64.

Morriss, L. (2016) 'Dirty secrets and being "strange": using ethnomethodology to move beyond familiarity', *Qualitative Research*, 16(5): 526–540.

Nelson-Miles, K. (2024) 'Micro-stories and meaning making in narrative research', in H. Kara (ed.), *The Bloomsbury Handbook of Creative Research Methods*, London: Bloomsbury, pp 71-82.

Owen Blakemore, J.E. and Centers, R.E. (2005) 'Characteristics of boys' and girls' toys', *Sex Roles*, 53(9/10): 619–633.

Parker, I. (1998) 'Against postmodernism: psychology in cultural context', *Theory & Psychology*, 8(5): 601–627.

Pauwels, L. (2011) 'An integrated conceptual framework for visual social research', in E. Margolis and L. Pauwels (eds), *The Sage Handbook of Visual Research Methods*, London: Sage, pp 3–23.

Pearson, M. and Wilson, H. (2019) 'Sandplay Therapy: A safe, creative space for trauma recovery', *Australian Counselling Research Journal*, 13(1): 20–24.

Pickering, M. (2008) 'Introduction', in M. Pickering (ed.), *Research Methods for Cultural Studies*, Edinburgh: Edinburgh University Press.

Pottinger, L., Barron, A., Hall, S.M., Ehgartner, U. and Browne, A.L. (2022) 'Talking methods, talking about methods: Invoking the transformative potential of social methods through animals, objects and how-to instructions', *GEO: Geography and Environment*, 9(1): https://doi.org/10.1002/geo2.107

Reddy, N. and Ratna, K. (2002) *A Journey in Children's Participation*, Vimanapura: The Concerned for Working Children, http://www.workingchild.org/prota9.htm

Rees, A., Staples, E. and Maxwell, N. (2017) *Final Report June 2017: Evaluation of Visiting Mum Scheme*, Cardiff: CASCADE.

Renold, E., Holland, S., Ross, N.J. and Hillman, A. (2011) '"Becoming participant": problematising "informed consent" in participatory research with young people in care', in P.A. Atkinson and S. Delamont (eds) *SAGE Qualitative Research Methods*, Vol. 4, London: Sage, pp 55–74.

Roberts, E. (2018), 'The "transient insider": identity and intimacy in home community research', in T. Loughran and D. Mannay (eds) *Emotion and the Researcher: Sites, Subjectivities, and Relationships*, Studies in Qualitative Methodology, Bingley: Emerald, pp 113–125.

Roberts, L., Rees, A., Bayfield, H., Corliss, C., Diaz, C., Mannay, D. et al (2020) *Young People Leaving Care, Practitioners and the Coronavirus (COVID 19) Pandemic: Experiences, Support, and Lessons for the Future*, Project Report, Cardiff: CASCADE/Cardiff University.

Rose, G. (2001) *Visual Methodologies: An Introduction to Researching with Visual Materials*, London: Sage.

Rose, G. (2016) *Visual Methodologies* (4th edn), London: Sage.

Sangganjanavanich, V.F. and S. Magnuson. (2011) 'Using sand trays and miniature figures to facilitate career decision making', *The Career Development Quarterly*, 59(3): 264–273.

Sheppard, L. (2018) '"Poor old mixed-up Wales": entering the debate about bilingualism, multiculturalism and racism in Welsh literature and culture', in T. Loughran and D. Mannay (eds) *Emotion and the Researcher: Sites, Subjectivities, and Relationships*, Studies in Qualitative Methodology, Bingley: Emerald, pp 197–212.

References

Silver, C., Bulloch, S.L. and Salmona, M. (2024) 'Digital tools for creative analysis: opportunities, challenges and future directions' in H. Kara (ed.), *The Bloomsbury Handbook of Creative Research Methods*, London: Bloomsbury, pp 31–46.

Smith, L.T. (2021) *Decolonizing Methodologies: Research and Indigenous Peoples* (3rd edn), London: Bloomsbury.

Staples, E.M., Watson, D. and Riches, K. (2024) 'Being, becoming, belonging: Negotiating temporality, memory and identity in life story conversations with care-experienced children and young people', *Qualitative Social Work*, 23(1): 67–89.

Taguchi, H.L. (2011) 'Investigating learning, participation and becoming in early childhood practices with a relational materialist approach', *Global Studies of Childhood*, 1(1): 36–50.

Tempone-Wiltshire, J. (2024) 'Sand talk: process philosophy and Indigenous knowledges', *Process Studies*, 53 (1): 42–68.

Thorne, S. (2000) 'Data analysis in qualitative research', *Evidence Based Nursing*, 3: 68–70.

Treloar, L. (2015) *Salt Creek*, London: Aardvark Bureau.

Turner, B.A. (2023) *The Handbook of Sandplay Therapy* (2nd edn), Petaluma, CA: Temenos Press.

Turney, C. (2021) *How Do Children Anticipate, Experience, and Manage the Transition from Primary to Secondary School?* PhD Thesis, Cardiff University.

Unwin, C. (1988) *Life of Margaret Lowenfeld*, Dr Margaret Lowenfeld Trust, https://lowenfeld.org/wp-content/uploads/2019/09/Life-of-Margaret-Lowenfeld-Cathy-Unwin.pdf

von Benzon, N. (2024) 'Human geography and creative methods: moving and mapping', in H. Kara (ed.), *The Bloomsbury Handbook of Creative Research Methods*, London: Bloomsbury, pp 48–58.

Ward, M.R.M. (2015) *From Labouring to Learning, Working-class Masculinities, Education and De-industrialization*, Basingstoke: Palgrave Macmillan.

Watson, D.L., Staples, E. and Riches, K. (2021) '"We need to understand what's going on because it's our life": Using sandboxing to understand children and young people's everyday conversations about care', *Children and Society*, 35(5): 663–679.

Wetherell, M. (2005) 'Unconscious conflict or everyday accountability?', *British Journal of Social Psychology*, 44(2): 169–173.

Woodcock, T. (1984) 'The use of the Lowenfeld Mosaic Test in child psychotherapy', *Projective Psychology*, 29(2): 11–18.

Yunkaporta, T. (2019) *Sand Talk: How Indigenous Thinking Can Save the World*, Melbourne: The Text Publishing Company.

Index

References to illustrations appear in *italic* type; those in **bold** type refer to tables. References to endnotes show both the page number and the note number.

A

auteur theory 3, 20, 49
Axline, Virginia 12–13, 14, 30, 79
  Dibs (case study) 12–13, 20

B

Bloor, Michael 54, 55–6
bodymapping 46
Broomfield, Katherine 50

C

case studies 7, 33–41, 42–8, 58–61, 62, 65, 81
children
  care-experienced and adopted children 40–1, 58–9, 70–4
  child psychotherapy 13, 14–15
  sandboxing and 2, 7, 39–41, 44–5, *45*, 47
  school transitions 46–8, 65, *65*
  see also play therapy; Visiting Mum scheme
Coffey, Julia 45–6
collages 3, 20, 42–3, 62, 85
  timeline collages 44, 48
coloured paper 16, 23, 65, 66, 67, 68
coloured/plain sticks 16, 24, 65
Computer Assisted Qualitative Data Analysis (CAQDAS) 51
creative research methods 2–3, 4, 5, 29–30, 43, 46, 47–8, 57, 83–4
  arts-based research 3, 53–4, 62
  data analysis 51–2
  researcher wellbeing and 55
  sandboxing as 6–7, 28
creativity 9–10

D

Dahal, Bibek 79
data analysis 27, 33, 51–2
data analysis (sandboxing) 7, 49–53
  different forms of 52–3
  meaning-making and interpretations by participants 49–50
  talk-based data 52
  thematic analysis 51, 52
  University Challenge project 25
data generation 27, 29, 41–2, 46, 85
  creative techniques of (other than sandboxing) 33
  ethical issues 25–8, 80
  objects and figures and 33–4
  sandboxing 20, 28, 29, 30–1, 33, 58, 61, 75
Davis, Madeleine 17
Difficult Conversations project 58–61, *60*, 75
disabilities, people with 2, 7, 51–2, 67, 81
doll's house 12–13
  museum study 57, 62–4, *64*, 75–6
Domestic Abuse Advocates (DAAs) 67–8
drawing 3, 11, 12, 17, 20, 47, 62, 84, 85
  timelines 48
Dumangane, Constantino Jr. 34–5

E

Eldén, Sara 43
elicitation interviews 40, 42, 43, 44, 46, 48, 49–50, 59, 62, 71
  objects and figures 7, 35–8, 56

ethical issues
  data generation 25–8, 80
  disclosures 41
  ethics *in situ* 28, 40, 80
  Lowenfeld, Margaret 28
  procedural ethics 39–40, 54, 55
  transferring therapeutic practice tools into qualitative research 7, 25–8, 80
ethnicity 67
'expressive sandwork' 20

F

free association 26, 27
Free Association Narrative Interview (FANI) 25–8
Freud, Anna 12, 14, 30, 79
Freud, Sigmund 11–12, 14, 26, 28, 30, 79
  psychosexual stages of development 12, 13–14, 87n2

G

Gautam, Suresh 79
glitter 16, 24, 65
Grant, Aimee 34, 42, 51

H

Haro, Adriana 38–9, 47, 81, 84
Harper, Douglas 50
Hart, Roger 29
Hodges, Amie 62
Holliday, Carol 39–40
Hollway, Wendy 25–7
Hurdley, Rachel 34

I

Indigenous communities
  Indigenous research 10, 30
  sand and 6, 10–11, 13, 30, 33, 79
  sandboxing and Indigenous knowledges 5, 9–11, 13, 79
  storytelling 6, 10–11
  yarning 10–11, 13
ink blots 11, 87n1
interior worlds 14, 18

J

Jefferson, Tony 25–7
Jung, Carl G. 19

K

Kalff, Dora 19–20, 79
  see also Sandplay

Kara, Helen 30, 49, 53, 57, 69, 70, 74
  Creative Research Methods in Practice Policy Press series 2, 5–6, 82
Klein, Melanie 12, 13, 14, 30, 79
Krzyżowski, Łukasz 55

L

LEGO® 3, 84, 85
Lisiak, Agata 55
Loughran, Tracey 53
Lowenfeld, Margaret 2, 9, 12, 13, 18, 30
  anthropology 19, 28
  child psychotherapy 13, 14–15
  children's thinking 15
  critique of 15–16, 18, 28
  educational research 19, 28
  ethical issues 28
  Mosaic Test 18–19
  play therapy/non-directive play 14, 20
  Poleidoblocs 19
  see also World Technique
Lytje, Martin 39–40

M

Maniatt, Rhiannon 37, 67, 83
Mannay, Dawn 1, 53, 62–4, 67, 70, 71, 74, 75–6
  sandboxing 20, 49
  see also sandboxing of the book; *University Challenge* project
Mannion, Jess 49, 51–2, 85
Mead, Margaret 18–19
metaphors/metaphoric quality 21, 42, 43, 59, 63, 67, 68, 74, 87n4
  benefits of sandboxing and 6, 23, 30, 62, 69, 81
'Methods for Change' project 83–4
Mosaic Approach 44
museum study 57, 62–4, *64*, 75–6

N

Nelson-Miles, Kim 52

O

objects and figures 7, 62, *73*
  benefits of working with 34–5, 39, 41
  bodymapping 46
  challenges related to 65–8, *68*, 83

Index

data generation and 33–4
Difficult Conversations project 59–61, 60
elicitation interviews 7, 35–8, 56
gender of figures 65–7
Indigenous knowledge and 10
internal narrative of images 3
modifying figures with craft materials 57, 65–8, 65, 76, 82
movement and change 35, 36, 37, 37–9, 38, 41, 50
participants' refusal to work with 34, 37
projects engagement, impact and dissemination 7–8, 57, 69–75, 76, 82
qualitative interviewing 34–5, 41
sand and 35–8, 41, 56
self-soothing 39, 41
'show' and 'tell' 37
size differences in sets of figures 67, 68
University Challenge project 21, 22–3, 23, 34, 35–6, 37, 65–6, 66, 68
Visiting Mum scheme 44–5, 45
World Technique 15–16, 57–8
see also doll's house; sandboxing; sandboxing of the book

P

Parker, Ian 26
participants
  involvement in design of research studies 41–2, 49
  meaning-making and interpretations by 49–50
  refusal to participate 48
  refusal to work with sand, objects and figures 34, 37
participatory research 29, 48
  'Ladder of Participation' 29
sandboxing 6–7, 29–30, 48, 49, 81
Piaget, Jean 14
Pickering, Michael 84–5
plasticine 16, 24, 48, 68, 85
  modifying figures with 47, 65, 65, 67, 76, 82
play therapy 12–13, 14
  non-directive play therapy 12, 14, 16, 20
  see also World Technique
Pottinger, Laura 83–4

Power, Nicki 54
pregnancy 42–3
psychoanalysis 2, 6, 9, 11–12, 13, 26, 30
sandboxing and 11, 13, 79, 80
psychoanalytically informed psychosocial inquiry 26, 27, 28
psychosocial research 26–8

Q

qualitative interviewing 2, 25–8, 45–6, 80, 82
  objects and figures 34–5, 41
  see also elicitation interviews; qualitative research
qualitative research 2, 4, 5, 11, 53, 83
  ethical issues 7, 25–8, 80
  sandboxing as 6, 20–5, 41, 75, 79, 82
  see also qualitative interviewing
queer Latinx men (Australia) 7, 38–9, 81, 84

R

R&S (Relationships and Sexuality) Research Team 49, 51–2
Rees, Alyson 43–5
Reggio Emilia philosophy 29
repression 11–12, 26
Research Excellence Framework (REF) Impact Case Study 70
research methods 57, 84–5
  collaborative approach 49, 51–2, 85
  Indigenous research 10, 30
  see also creative research methods; participatory research; psychosocial research; qualitative research; sandboxing
researchers 69–70
  positionality of 40, 53
  sandboxing 40, 42–3, 48
  wellbeing of 7, 53–6
  see also vicarious trauma
Riches, Katie 58
Robinson, Stephen 49
Rorschach, Hermann 87n1
Rose, Gillian 3, 20, 49, 50, 69, 74

S

sand 77–8
  alternatives to sand in sandboxing 49
  Indigenous communities/knowledges and 6, 10–11, 13, 30, 33, 79
  objects, figures and 35–8, 41, 56

105

participants' refusal to work with 37
therapeutic practice and 13
water and 15, 57
'Sand Talk' 10–11, 33, 79
sand tray therapy 2, 13, 19–20, 79
  see also World Technique
sandboxing 2
  challenges 48, 61, 70–1
  collaboration and co-production 7
  as creative research 6–7, 28
  data generation 20, 28, 29, 30–1, 33, 58, 61, 75
  ethical issues 25–8
  Indigenous knowledges and 5, 9–11, 13, 79
  as methodological tool 28
  as participatory research 6–7, 29–30, 48, 49, 81
  as planning and design tool for writing projects 69, 76
  psychoanalysis and 11, 13, 79, 80
  as qualitative research 6, 20–5, 41, 75, 79, 82
  relational qualities of 77–9
  therapeutic practice and 6, 11, 13, 79, 80
  World Technique and 13, 20–1, 23–5, 28, 30, 58, 79
  see also data analysis (sandboxing); objects and figures
sandboxing: adaptions 7, 57, 75–6, 82
  crafting equipment 24
  doll's house 57, 62–4, *64*, 75–6
  modifying figures with craft materials 57, 65–8, *65*, 76, 82
  water 24, 57–61, *60*, 75, 82
sandboxing: benefits and risks 41
  anonymity for participants 7–8, 28, 57, 70–2
  children 41, 45, 61–2
  creation and communication of experiences 30, 36, 45, 62, 69
  creation of space to think and reflect 59, 69
  emotional engagement 28, 37
  flexibility and adaptability 36, 81
  metaphors/metaphoric quality of sandboxing 6, 23, 30, 62, 69, 81
  projects engagement, impact and dissemination 7–8, 57, 69–75, 76, 82
  unintended/unexpected journeys for participants and researchers 28, 54, 55
  water, benefits from the use of 59–61
sandboxing: recommendations 77, 83–5
  planning and contingency measures 84
sandboxing kits 48–9, 68, 83, 85
  University Challenge project 21, 24, 35, 65–6, 68
  see also objects and figures
sandboxing of the book 3–6, *4*, 76, 77–82, *78*, 83, 85
sandboxing with other techniques 41–9, 56, 81, 85
  see also bodymapping; collages; drawing; plasticine; timelines; word bubble
Sandplay 19, 79, 87n3
Staples, Eleanor 58
storytelling 6, 10–11, 34
subjective knowledge 11

T

Taguchi, Hillevi Lenz 77–8
talking therapy 11
therapeutic practice 5, 30
  creative and visual activities and 11, 12
  sandboxing and 6, 11, 13, 79, 80
  see also play therapy
therapists 14
  non-directive play therapy 12, 14
  World Technique 16–17, 20
  see also vicarious trauma
timelines 42–3, 47–8, 85
  timeline collages 44, 48
Timperley, Vicky (née Edwards) 1
  see also sandboxing of the book; University Challenge project
Tinkerbell toys 21, 35, 65–6, *66*, 80, 82
Treloar, Lucy 55
Turner, Barbara A. 19
Turney, Catt 46–8, 49, 65, 81

U

'Umpan' 11
the unconscious 9, 11–12, 14, 18, 26, 27, 58

University Challenge project 2, 4, 20,
    30–1, 80
  data analysis 25
  objects and figures 21, **22–3**, 23,
    34, 35–6, *37*, 65–6, *66*, 68
  participants 24–5
  sand/sand tray kit 21, 24, 35,
    65–6, 68
  Tinkerbell figure 35, 65–6, *66*,
    80, 82

V

vicarious trauma 37, 54, 55, 67
Visiting Mum scheme 43–5, *45*

W

water
  Difficult Conversations project 59–61,
    60, 75
  sand and 15, 57
  sandboxing and 24, 57–61, *60*,
    75, 82

World Technique 15, 24, 57–8,
    61, 75, 80
Watson, Debbie 58
word bubble 42, 43
World Technique 2, 6, 9, 15–18,
    19, 30, 58
  critique of 15–16, 18
  developments and adaptions 18–20
  equipment 15–16, 23–4, 58,
    64–5, 67
  objects and figures 15–16, 57–8
  sandboxing and 13, 20–1, 23–5,
    28, 30, 58, 79
  'symbolization', meaning and
    interpretation 16–17, 20
  therapists 16–17, 20
  water 15, 24, 57–8, 61, 75, 80
  see also Lowenfeld, Margaret

Y

yarning 10–11, 13
Yunkaporta, Tyson 10–11